SIMPLIFIED TAX
SYSTEM

SIMPLIFIED TAX SYSTEM

◆

A Counterculture Proposal

Lawrance George Lux

iUniverse, Inc.
New York Lincoln Shanghai

SIMPLIFIED TAX SYSTEM
A Counterculture Proposal

iUniverse, Inc.

For information address:
iUniverse, Inc.
2021 Pine Lake Road, Suite 100
Lincoln, NE 68512
www.iuniverse.com

ISBN: 0-595-30648-9

Printed in the United States of America

Contents

Foreword

This attempt may turn into 'Devine Comedy', as does most endeavors entered into with limited resources. The entire Process of Taxation in the modern sense has become complex, the Individual having little ability to make complete sense of it; there are always extraneous elements required for consideration. The sheer magnitude of the effort required not only a Statement defining the Tax imposed, but also an Economic rationale for the imposition. Modern Tax Systems cover the entire gambit of Economic participation. This Author will undoubtedly leave himself open to ridicule by both Professional Tax Assessor and Lay Person. Reevaluation needs of current Tax Systems remain obvious; the Nation is sinking into Debt—both Public and Private, incentive programs and tax credits exceed the boundaries of rational analysis, and Tax Escape vies with Tax Rape with few Taxpayers immune from the ill effects. The final vitality must be the limitation of Government expenditure, which has been allowed free rein, as watchdog Taxpayers are diverted into a search of Tax credits and Deductions.

This book will be written, hopefully, maintaining certain basic precepts which the Author understands to be mandatory for the improvement of the current Tax Code. The first basic premise states that the Tax Code must be unified; Our modern Economy can no longer endure a multiplicity of tax rates brought through Local, State, and Federal taxation. Constitutional amendment cannot, and should not be used. The alternative is writing suitable legislation. This must be done on the Federal level, in order for the entirety of the Tax System to be subjected to the change.

The second precept requires a definition of Tax Policy, the purported end of Tax legislation. Tax Policy must state a primary goal. A number of goals can be entertained: the promotion of Economic growth (GDP), the promotion of Business needs, the promotion of Employment, the promotion of Labor welfare, the promotion of Social Welfare, the promotion of redistribution of Income, and the promotion of Individual Liberty. The Reader will have noticed the usage of the word 'promotion' repeatedly, as this is the end-game of Policy of any type. The Author will diverge from all of the above, noting that promotion of One of the initiatives necessarily suppresses all of the rest in implementation extremis. The Author opts for another value called the promotion of the Standard of Living.

Many Tax advocates proclaim a need for Equality of Taxation. This stands as a totally inapplicable proposition. Genuine equality of Taxation would insist no one should pay any more than any other. Business should pay exactly the same as any Individual, and it turns into nothing more than a Head Tax limited by the ability to Pay, of the most disadvantaged in society. This would result in the Government remaining unfunded. Most claim Tax should be assessed on the basis of ability to Pay. This process justification, though, eliminates all operative power to grant Exemptions, Deductions, and Tax credits; even introducing the concept of Expenses reduces Equality, unless every Taxpayer receives only a like Expenses allowance. Neither Business nor Individual could survive, when all are limited to a set level of Capital utilization. All Tax Systems may achieve only a rude Tax balance, more crudely termed: the ability to pay without undue distress.

The third precept outlines need for limitation of the 'Boom and Bust Cycle', which huants Economics. This Cycle derives from the nature of human participation in the Economy. Individuals tend to overspend, both in Consumption and in Investment. They also manage all economic elements of the Economy, carrying their practices of over-expenditure along with them. They will invest to the degree their economic Consumption is impaired, then when their investments start to derive Profits and other Payments; they will feel rich, and will tend to over-consume until their ability to invest is lost. This is not a serious consideration within the context of Individual behavior, but disastrous in aggregate grouping. Economics relates the fact there must be a balance between Consumption and Investment in order to minimize Busts and lengthen Booms.

The Author has inherent belief that Tax Burden must be placed upon the Consumers under Bust conditions, and be switched to Business Profits under Boom conditions. Most Economists consider this statement to be heresy. The Government must become the major Investor under recessive conditions, investing in Infrastructure, utilizing mandatory contributions from Consumers by Taxation. Government expenditures should decrease under Boom conditions, but Tax Burden should be placed on Business Profits, to enhance both the Consumption and Savings of Consumers. There are obvious defects to this program, most coming from the political tendency to spend government revenues where they exist, alongside a reluctance to pressure Voters into a severe Savings ratio under recessionary conditions. This does not make the Initiative impossible. It simply calls for proper Tax empowerment.

The fourth precept relates to the Proper Choice theory of Economics. This theory insists self-interest governs Government legislation, while Public or communal interests suffer. The Author stands in total agreement with this statement, though not with the proscriptions to forestall the aforementioned self-interest, as advanced by these Economists. The Author advocates a Constitutional amendment stating no legislation can be passed into law can be more than fifty booklength pages in length, must be in legible language which any college graduate could read and understand, and must be constrained to one topic; violation of any of the prior conditions will lead to automatic dismissal by Federal courts as unconstitutional. An additional addendum will state the legislative vote by name must be appended to the document. Logrolling would be limited by this amendment. A further condition of the Amendment could be stated that if Congress and President cannot agree to a current Year Budget by September 1 of each Year, then the previous Year's budget must be used for the current Year, and no Legislative Law of the current Year can be implemented without funding.

There are currently thirteen separate Appropriations Budgets considered by Congress and President. Each of these Appropriations should be broken into separate bills: composed of Beneficiaries Appropriations, Civil Service personnel Appropriations, Capitalization Appropriations, Maintenance Appropriations, Research Appropriations, and Employee Retirement appropriations. The Above Constitutional amendment should insist all these limited Appropriations be examined by the Federal Courts to eliminate special groups' privileges from the legislation, using the context of inordinate gain for special interests, effectively giving the Courts an 'Item Veto' solely to maintain equivalence of Citizen treatment under the Law. Tax Policy should equally be governed by this Amendment; it stating discrimination between Taxpayers allowed solely due to level of Income. This provision will constrain efforts to promote Economic policies through discrimination, and adequately limit Government expenditures.

The fifth precept used will be the belief Government utilization of Economic policy can be as incitive of recessionary conditions, as it can be a promotion of economic growth. Liberal Welfare Economics vies with Supply-Side Economists; the first group claiming there should be welfare programs to redistribute Wealth, the second viewing the promotion of Business as the only positive method to promote economic growth. The Author disagrees with both Schools, for the Record.

Welfare programs only develop growth of bureaucracy in Government, and growth of program-Providers in the Private sector. This growth consists of new participation in the Economy, and will eventually absorb all funds allocated to intended Beneficiaries; they are left in their prior position, due to their lack of participation in the economy. An excellent case in point is the Medicare program; most beneficiaries left with less ability to pay for their medical care as they possessed in 1966, at the start of the Medicare program. This has come about due to the administrative costs of the Social Security administration, the administration costs of Medical Providers, in addition to increased costs of the Medical provision itself. Housing Assistance is also vulnerable to retention of inferior Housing, and vastly increased rents for that Housing, alongside a huge increase in administrative costs in the program. Economic benefit cannot be transferred effectively, without the participation of the Beneficiaries in the Economy.

The argument to promote Business activity by tax incentives and protective legislation is equally as flawed. The reality of a modern banking system does cancel the aggregation of capital function, so normally used by Economists as rationale for tax incentive and tax credits, especially with the presence of large, already-capitalized Business enterprise. The Author is not an advocate of internal financing for Business growth, most notably for Corporations. Outside financing provides an extensive review process by the Lender, who insists the Borrower does the proper research and investigation for the proposed Loan. Most internally-financed Business endeavors lack at least one-third of the required research, and shows a resulting lack of Market or reasonable Production Costs Schedules. Large Corporations often dispense with any Research at all, singularly wanting to employ funds which would otherwise be taxed. The resulting losses of Profitability are charged to other efficient Production operations of the Business organization.

Business protective legislation brings carelessness to business operations, as they deliberately violate Safety and Environmental concerns in the interest of higher Profits. Corporations have knowingly dumped hazardous wastes, well aware of the danger to local human populations and environments. The current Administration has allowed them to continue to emit pollutants at rates which are hazardous to the environment, and which had previously been regulated. Ineffective Court punitive damages against Business, allow them to operate adverse operations at a Profit, and deduct the minimal cost of the Damage awards from their Taxes by act of Government. Conformance to Health, Safety, and Environmental standards will only come with effective punishment for Business transgressions.

The entire policy of Business favoritism contains error. Business management becomes sloppy, when they conceive that Government will bail them out at the first sign of trouble. A noticeable cause of Outsourcing of Product to Overseas production comes from disinclination to oversee Production. Management is protected from Civil liability, does not find need to supervise Production for efficiency or Product quality, and does not even need to commit to a policy of heavy Sales; Management can still derive Profits by tax credits, and elimination of an internal labor force. At least half of the evaporation of Jobs in this Country has come from the sheer laziness of Business management, who can maintain Profits without labor through Government-sponsored Protections and Tax advantages. Any Tax System must change this Parasitism cultivated by Government legislation. The American Economy loses economic viability in the World, not from the inadequacy of Labor, but from the inadequacy of Management, fostered by Government policy.

The paramount element to be considered in any Tax System must consist of the current National Debt, created by excessive Government expenditures and lax Tax policy. The Author has previously tried to convey through his Writings that the National Debt is the leading Suppressant of Consumption, due to absorption of Resources and Production facilities, without actually paying for that usage by Taxation. Most Economists witness this overinflation of Production facilities, and claim it is good for Economic performance. It is actually quite harmful!

Such Expenditure without Taxes becomes a simple creation of Money, based upon no economic effort—Inflation. The Inflation appears as Resource price increases, and Consumer price increases for both Business and Final-Product Consumer. The financing or Service of the Debt entails payment of Interest on the Debt, again insisting on the creation of Money based upon no economic effort. Continued Deficit spending produces reduction of value of Profits of Private Production, requiring Business to insist on higher Profits, causing them to suppress compensation to Labor—further reducing Consumption. The Inflationary funds created mix with economically-sound Money supplies; all Funds insisting on a rate of return, so all funds are devalued along with their rate of return. The Money Supply is not only inflated, but corrupted in that non-productive Product with no rate of return has been produced. This element means the cost of Infrastructure to the total Economy has increased, with increased Recapitalization costs without increases in Productivity.

Serious measures must be taken to eliminate Government deficits, and further; serious effort must be made to pay off the existing National Debt. Service of the Debt still creates artificial Money through the payment of Interest on the Debt. A Tax System which does not fulfil this need stands as ineffective. Almost all Economists unite against this proposition, citing the huge size of the Debt with reciprocating necessary high rates of taxation, coupled with proclaimed loss of economic incentive from elimination of tax advantages for Business. It remains the responsibility of Advocacy, to define a Tax System which will fulfil all needs while maintaining economic performance. Laughter is allowed at this point, but please read on.

SECTION I

Chapter 1

The first Initiative must be to unify the Tax Code of this Country. The multiplicity of tax rates—Federal, State, and Local—cannot endure, this not only because of the long-term inequality of tax incidences, but also due to the diminishment of economic performance engendered in the Economy. Differences of tax incidences produce disparities in Labor wages by area, effectively determining Rents, Product pricing, and Business cost in the area. This affects not only the viability of industry in the area, to sell outside the area in question, it produces disparities in Government welfare programs in the area. Local areas find themselves priced out of the Labor market due to Business portability, or inundated with Business investment which exceeds the capacity to provide basic Services; leading to adverse increases in Utilities cost, Transportation costs, Education costs, and Housing costs. The latter affected area must rapidly raise Taxes, paying for Services, and leading to an evacuation of Business; or acquire their own local Government debt burden. The former area suffers from loss of tax revenues, along with an aging population which requires extensive Welfare programs.

It has had previously been mentioned the unconstitutional nature of constraining the Budgetary powers of subordinate levels of Government, which would include the powers to tax. The separation of levels of Government is sacrosanct in American political heritage. A less drastic situation methodology can be devised, utilizing powers of the Federal government to regulate the national economy, united with their power to tax.

The first basic tenant of the new Tax System need be carefully crafted to insure no level of government will be constrained in their exercise of legitimate power, without insert crippling the superior level of government. The basic provision would read something like the following:

The basic Federal form of Taxation will be an Income Tax. Income, for Individual or Business organization, will be any form of compensation of any type, one which allows the entity to be an Economic Participant. The only exemptions will be Welfare transfer payments made by Government action, below a certain monetary maximum determined by Congress on a

yearly basis. All levels of Government retain all right and power to impose further taxes as they feel fit, but such taxes will be seen as entity exemption from assessed Federal Income tax. The Federal Government reserves the right to provide additional Personnel exemptions and tax credits to all subject to taxation, as long as they are uniform in nature. Normal reductions of assessed Income tax will remain in force to allow for normal Business expenses and unusual circumstances for specific classes of Taxpayers.

All Income tax rates will be uniform for all entities, and determined by act of Congress, with consent of the President, or override of a Veto. Such Income tax rates will be determined once a year in the normal Budget passage process. The Federal government reserves the right to violate the uniformity of the exemption of subordinate level taxes, with supplanting percentage rates of exemption of subordinate taxes; if Congress determines, some subordinate jurisdiction assesses taxes above the average or mean of all subordinate jurisdiction rates of taxation.

The above formulation accomplishes many things. The rest of this Chapter will be an examination of those changes, so the Reader can evaluate the value of such changes.

The definition of Income presented differs from the current usage of the term. Income, as defined by Congressional act today, is separated from many forms of alternate acquisition of funds, basically, on the general basis of Investment returns. Profits from Capital Gains, Rents, Royalties, and Copyrights are currently defined separate from Income, allowing for differentiation of tax rates. This separation is fundamentally illusionary in nature, simply an administrative act for the purpose of gaining tax advantage.

The major rationale for the above separation is allowance to avoid the progressive nature of the Income Tax law currently in force. A simple translation of the previous statement states wealthy or stationed entities does not want to pay a higher percentage tax, for the sole reason they have earned more; even though the Income Tax law insists that Labor be subjected to such progressive taxation. All Economic Participants utilize gained funds to finance their economic participation. The split among forms of Income turned the Income Tax law currently in force into a regressive tax; where Labor must pay higher taxes for Income earned, than does established wealth, which earns a return on that wealth. There is no difference in the utilization of the Income, no matter how derived; Labor expresses equal incentive to Save and Invest, when allowed the excess funds to do so.

Prominent Economic arguments assert wealth-derived gains cannot be progressively taxed, because it would inhibit the aggregation of capital assets. Economists supportive of the argument do not separate actual construction of Production land, equipment, and organization from the acquirement of financial liquidity. This distinction is not made because it would express the irrelevance of the distinction. There are two possibilities for actual Productive Capital construction, known commonly as Hard Capitalization, the first consisting of internal financing of hard construction by Business and Corporation, the second through utilization of loans from financial institutions. Internal financing of hard construction often lacks oversight as mentioned previously, while the basic components of capital aggregation by financial institutions remain Demand Deposits (in which Certificates of Deposit, of Timed Deposits, are included).

The aggregation of Capital through Demand Deposits does not insist on large or small deposits, only the total aggregate of deposits. The financial institutions are independent of the Savings ratio, deriving their power to aggregate, whether their Depositors express a high ratio of Savings or Spendthrifts; it is only necessary they deposit their funds in the interim between earning it and spending it. There would be some shortfalls if Depositors were in every sense only Consumers, leaving their funds only until they could spend it. This defect, though, is minimized by the uniform pattern of deposits, and sponsorship of the Federal Reserve Bank, which provides funds as necessary at good reinvestment rates of interest.

The necessity of separating Capital Gains from Labor Income remains fiction. Corporate and Business structure implements hard capital construction prior to dispersal of Profits. The central banking system utilizes a separate aggregate function other than individual savings to aggregate necessary capital. Income separation for purposes of taxation simply protects wealthy elements of society; they would otherwise face identical progressive taxation alongside Labor. There will be protest from Stock and Bond markets, but only because of lower commissions, and because their Clientele will feel victimized by paying an equivalent tax with Labor.

The second major element of the stated Tax provision unifies the Tax System of this Country, by establishing subordinate taxes paid to subordinate jurisdictions are direct reductions of the final tax assessment, considered identical to Business expense for all Taxpayers. The ability of Congress to set percentage limits of said exemption for entities under subordinate jurisdiction which inordinately tax, will allow for a uniformity of Tax incidences to be placed upon all. The Taxpayers, who suffer from a percentage of the exemption because of excessive Local, State, or Federal taxes, will pressure subordinate jurisdictions for Tax relief at that level. The hazards of Proper Choice Economics are amended by increased Public participation, through direct impact upon their Incomes.

Subjecting all Income-Earners to the same progressive taxation will lead to a normalization of basic Costs to all Households and Industries, no matter where located. There are no avenues left open, where escape of progressive taxation is viable. The most important element of this transition is in reintroduction of justified Recapitalization practices, where Business and Landlord do not enjoy as much gain by running their physical Plant into the ground. Plant is the economic term for Properties which is Income producing. Justified Recapitalization practice is the upkeep of Plant to maximize complete use of Asset value. Rent-gouging, burn-up Profits-taking, and marketing of inferior Product all become less Profitable, when progressive taxation of Profits is introduced.

The Federal government can tax some types of Government Welfare transfers, whether they are Federal dispersals, or when they have been provided by subordinate governments. This is an important tool for the equalization of benefits, and for reduction of area living costs to the national average. Equalization of benefits remains important as American Citizens should benefit in equal measure, for the taxes paid by all Citizens; it is call Economic parity of Government Welfare. It is another tool to regulate excess Cost of Living expenses in subordinate areas, without providing extreme adversity to Recipients of such Transfer payment; few, if any, would pay more than the basic bottom tax rate. Landlords and Utilities, along with Retailers, would realize unrealistic pricing for their Product will only generate animosities, not sustainable Profits, this due to increasing delays of payment. The Federal Government can equally set tax rates, so that a base level of Income is not taxed at all.

The uniformity of taxation on all forms of Income serves a vital purpose, and this related to Proper Choice Economics. Taxpayers will be excluded from seeking major tax reductions by special class or Grouping. They will have to resort to overall suppression of tax rates, as uniformity of taxation removes most of the discrimination from taxation. This brings unity to Taxpayers, with objections to the extremity of tax rates, at all three levels of jurisdiction. Politicians will find less capacity to remove pressures against excessive expenditures, by discrimination against specific classes of Taxpayers. Informed Taxpayers will be induced to bring uninformed Taxpayers into a general opposition to growth of Government, with eventual concurrent increased Taxation. The principles of Proper Choice are served.

Later elements of this Work will deal with the issue of tax credit. It is sufficient to say their revision will aid in implementation of Proper Choice principles. These will bring Business organization into the camp of individual Taxpayers, so that Proper Choice will become a watchword of Private Sector participation in Politics. Individuals and organizations should not fear the following text, as it is not the intent of the Author to impoverish any Taxpayer, or even to redistribute Wealth. The sole intent is to rationalize the Tax System, a necessary precondition, prior to reorganization of Government, vital in finally stopping the expansion of Government spending. People, who can achieve their own financial goals, do not need or want Government intrusion.

The current system of Government stands in complete defiance of Popular rule. Lobbyists and Special Interests have destroyed all coherency to Government action. They did so with the expectation they would compose a privileged Class. They even find current Government operation chaotic and ineffective, matched with an expense from which even the Wealthy are beginning to suffer. The only thing, which approximates the growth of the National Debt, consists of extorted political campaign contributions. Federal borrowing, combined with State and Local deficits, is stripping the financial liquidity from the American economy. The switch of Tax incidences to the Consumer already brings serious reduction to Consumption levels. Conflicting Federal, State, and Local demands nullify Business advantages gained through huge Lobbying expenditures. Politicians always extend more hands to be paid. Expenses continue to rise for all Taxpayers, and the Government only suggests more programs which must be funded by Tax revenues or deficits. Real change only comes when the system is breaking down, so it is impossible to gain special advantage from it. There is where American Government is Today!

Chapter 2

The Income Tax System remains plagued with the complexity of human relationships. A straight Income Tax would ignore these relationships, and tax everyone equally. This seems ideal, but leads to serious disparity in actual impact upon Households. Congress has been trying to establish an equitable viability to Income Tax since its inception. No real solution has been achieved, though there is a plentitude of allowed Deductions which join Personal Exemptions. Their interaction, though, tends to produce disparity; with higher Incomes enjoying greater advantage, than do lower Incomes. The Solution is to eliminate them all, but within a context containing acceptance of different abilities to pay.

The Author will again present a possible Tax Provision to possibly cure the disparities of ability to pay a common tax. This Provision will probably remain the most controversial, at least in terms of effect:

> The basic Federal form of Taxation will be an Income Tax. Income, for Individual or Business organization, will be any form of compensation of any type, which allows the entity to be an Economic Participant. The only exemptions will be Welfare transfer payments made by Government action, below a certain monetary maximum determined by Congress on a yearly basis. All levels of Government retain all right and power to impose further taxes as they feel fit, but such taxes will be seen as entity exemption from assessed Federal Income tax. The Federal Government reserves the right to provide additional Personal exemptions and tax credits to all subject to taxation, as long as they are uniform in nature. Normal reductions of assessed Income tax will remain in force to allow for normal Business expenses and unusual circumstances for specific classes of Taxpayers.
>
> All Income tax rates will be uniform for all entities, and determined by act of Congress, with consent of the President, or override of a Veto. Such Income tax rates will be determined once a year in the normal Budget passage process. The Federal government reserves the right to violate the uniformity of the exemption of subordinate level taxes, with supplanting percentage rates of exemption of subordinate taxes; if Congress determines, some subordinate jurisdiction assesses taxes above the average or mean of all subordinate jurisdiction rates of taxation.

The Reader can understand why Tax Code legislation often turns into books resembling a Dictionary. Several administrative decisions will have to be allowed, such as OMB must be allowed to estimate, or use a 12-month Period ending three months previous to the release of Tax Schedules, to allow time for computation. It still seems like a genuine improvement from current practice.

Examination of the Provision provides a list of what it accomplishes, and what it does not. The first element discards literally decades of Congressional dispensations for specific groups subject to taxation. The simple discard of bad law brings simplification to the Tax Code, and removes complex restrictions on how taxable Income is to be determined. Individual Households need not keep complex records of receipts, bills, welfare transfers, and various other determinants. Internal Revenue personnel surrenders the need to closely check itemized deductions. Tax Returns can be simplified: with fewer input notations on which mistakes can be made, along with less confusing language. The Economist would say the Cost of Tax routing will have reduced, as well as the Cost of Tax Collection.

The yearly survey conducted by the Office of Management and Budget will supply a wealth of information for Economists, and provide Congress with the material to assess the impact of the Tax Code, allowing the institution to modify tax rates adequately. Government can utilize the information to determine the effectiveness of welfare transfer payment, along with the impact of Social programs. Disparities among Households can be determined for future Social action, and regrettably, Business also able to efficiently target Households for Advertising.

The averaging of the separate Costs of Living for each level of taxable Income serves a recognized Wealth transfer program, and much hated by Conservatives. Lower Incomes are given a larger Cost of Living allowance exemption than their actual Costs would warrant, while Higher Incomes would receive a lower Cost of Living allowance exemption less than their actual Costs dictate. The Cost of Living allowance exemption would likely approximate the progressive scale of the Income tax itself, with the Dependent allowance exemption seems likely to improve on the wealth transfer nature of the Income Tax itself.

The Extraordinary Expense allowance exemptions serve as excellent vehicle for welfare assistance, without resorting to expensive legislation and welfare program instillation. The individual Taxpayer can seek Private Sector assistance in terms of loans, with insistence the excess expenses grant him the allowance exemption, this empowering his ability to make repayments. It also allows him to pay residual bills are they come due, and insures personal underwriting of adverse costs. The lack of Government intervention in most circumstances of such type, probably saves the Government an equal amount as lost in the exemption, due to freedom from program service. The Economist often has to prove to the Layperson that a simple solution is far less costly than a bureaucratic plan. We all have to prove this fact to the Politicians.

The misery of Joint Returns will reduce from this Provision. Joint Income Households provide such misery because disparity between Income levels of Household Earners often cut half the deserved tax rate (real tax, or the actual taxes which should have been paid for the Income level). The new Joint Return would insist each Income Earner would receive only the Cost of Living allowance exemption current with their own Income level of taxation, while the Household could pay the combination of tax of each level of Income, or the alternative level of the combined Income of the Household. This assessment will anger most married couples; in actuality, it only closes a tax loophole established for married couples.

Married couples will be mollified by the reality of Cost of Support for Dependent allowance exemption, which functionally allows for tax relief more in line with the actual cost of Child-rearing. It also serves another valuable function, as it relieves some of the burden of Dependency from the Individual, and placing it on the Community. Taxpayers feel less excluded from the largesse granted to Welfare-assisted children, as the personal costs of their own children are adequately reflected in the Tax Code. Lower Income parentage is expected to provide all the elements of Child-rearing, as does the Government in Welfare relief for Children; yet, their financial resources are severely constrained. Their children often must live at inferior Standard of Living, because they are not underwritten by Government resources. A more equitable Cost of Dependents exemptions reverses this trend.

The true value for the Economist in the Provision stands as elimination of need for funded Welfare programs, as the Tax Code would handle all but the Indigent. The lower Income classes are allowed Tax relief through enhanced Personal Exemption and Dependent allowance, while upper Income classes find a progressive reduction in their own Exemptions based solely the magnitude of their Income. Costly exterior Government social programs stand limited to only those who cannot find work. This reduces the cost of Government funding immeasurably, as Civil Service funding needs reduce, and through avoidance of Beneficiary budgetary funding. The Welfare assistance is built into the Tax Code itself.

Tax Code rates can also be constructed with allows freedom from taxation below a certain level of Income. This stands as a very poor idea! Extreme use grants excessive ability to evade taxation, by segments of society which should pay taxes. Americans detest the concept of forcing poor people to pay taxes, thinking it is a form of Tax-gouging. Simple introduction of the idea of taxing the Poor will bring some animosity for the Author, but later explanations in this Work will explain the need. The amounts under discussion here extend to no more than $200bn per year; with realizable tax generation of no more than $15bn per year; but it integrates the Tax Code, cancels tax evasions, and clarifies the Tax base upon which taxes are drawn. The three reasons stated will generate greater revenue for the Government, than will the actual taxes upon the Poor. The only requirement consists of writing a proper Tax Code, where the Poor are not injured unduly(taxed within the parameters of their Standard of Living). Latter efforts will outline how this can be done.

Chapter 3

Current Tax law places Taxes for Unemployment Insurance, Social Security, and various other Welfare programs outside of Income taxation. The rationale for this lies in that they feed various maintained Fund budgets, separate from the General Revenue budget of the Federal government. A secondary goal of this separation remains a limitation of what economic units are subject to tax. This later Concept seems rationale, but is it? This Chapter will explore the rationality of taxing a certain class for the benefit of another class, after another Tax provision is outlined:

> **Special Fund Budgets will remain defined, but taxation for such Budgets will be integrated into the Income Tax and Income Tax rates. Congress will vote yearly, within Appropriations legislation, how much of the General Revenues shall be diverted to fund the Special Budgets.**

Special Fund Budgets habitually fail to meet the necessity's fulfillment for which the Funds were established. The economic rationales for this factor states Fund Budgets cannot borrow like a separate economic entity, and therefore; it can only achieve permanent parity with necessity payments, only through excessive tax rates in the initial phase. A more evolved Economic argument states the Special Fund Budgets must meet national economic goals, but are limited to special class taxation; either the special classes are overtaxed, or Fund shortages are accrued over time in Fund Budget operation.

Unemployment Insurance may be the easiest to analyze, though the Social Security Fund will be discussed later. The national goal of Unemployment Insurance guarantees Employees, who lose their jobs, have some form of assistance until they can find alternate employment, whether that loss of a job is permanent, or only a temporary layoff. Business has been nominated as a special class, who was to finance this Fund through special taxation, an endurance of a new Operating Cost, in the form of a tax for a Welfare program. The national goal was sound, but the source of funding was not. Tax withdrawals from Business had to be excessive, or the Fund Budget would empty too quickly in recessionary times. The Operating Cost to fund a Welfare program becomes too onerous during recessionary times, and deepens the recessionary effects. Smaller Tax withdrawals come in during recessionary conditions, it also means smaller Tax revenues in boom conditions. Business need endure excessive taxation in both Boom and Bust cycles, and the Unemployment Fund Budget is habitually drained of funds anyway.

The Social Security Fund Budget stands deeply in the Black today; so Black, Government strips it of funds for the General revenues constantly, so they can provide Tax Cuts elsewhere. Most Readers possess some understanding after constant debate on the Issue, that the SS Fund Budget stays in the Black solely because of the ratio of Workers to Beneficiaries. Many Workers pay into the SS Fund Budget, while a substantially smaller number draw Benefits from it. The amounts of benefit granted by the program both increase in number and Cost. Readers recognize the ratio of Workers to Beneficiaries will reduce drastically with the retirement of the Baby Boomer Generation, of which the Author is one. The actuality will place the purported SS Fund Budget, whose resources have already been drained, directly in the Red or Deficit, without sharply increasing Tax withdrawals.

The above paragraph tells us many things. The greatest element to be realized must be that Congress and President is already using SS Tax withdrawals as Income taxes, for use in sustaining the Federal budget, this in order to reduce Business taxes, and restrain a heavier tax burden on the Wealthy. The era of Baby Boomer retirement will not be funded even partially by the SS Fund Budget, because it has already effectively been spent by Congress and President. Their retirement can only be funded by heavier taxation on the remaining Workers, whether through heavier Social Security Tax withdrawals or increased rates of Income taxation. The Reader may recognize the American Economy ploughs ahead into financial disaster. The only solution can be revision of the current Tax Code.

Tax Code theory should be brought into the analysis at this Point, along with some use of Proper Choice Economics. Current Tax Code relies on political evasion, to provide for tax evasion. Congress, President, and Special Interests are left free to pursue their own self-interest, without facing the consequences of their actions. Special Fund Budgets exist only as empty Accounting procedures, empty Funds, or inadequate reserves. None will operate as designed without ingestion of new tax revenues. The manner in which those tax revenues are raised will affect the responsibility level expressed by Congress and President.

Integration of Special Fund Budget tax withdrawals into the general Income tax rates will have great beneficial effects. Americans realize they want the Special

Fund Budgets to operate as designed, meaning they positively desire for these Funds to be financed, while they enjoy far less desire to allow Special Interests access to tax evasion procedures. Incorporations of Special Fund Budget tax withdrawals into the general Income tax rates serve two purposes. The First compels the Income tax rates be sufficient to fund operation of the Special Fund Budgets which American Citizens desire most. The Second causation insists Congress and President are yearly held responsible for maintaining finance of these Special Fund Budgets, so that services provided are maintained. A secondary effect of this integration incites a limitation upon Congress and President to limit Discretionary spending by themselves, as they must enter either Deficit spending or raise Income Tax rates.

Economists will rejoice at such integration as well. The tax burden for a national welfare transfer system of extreme proportions transmits from a limited Taxpayer base, onto a much larger Taxpayer base. Down to Earth Readers may prefer the explanation of the tax burden being shifted from Business and Labor, onto the entirety of Participants in the Economy. Business and Labor have to pay a lesser share of the tax, enhancing their viability of economic participation, especially during recessionary times. These Special Fund Budgets become less of a complete Welfare transfer system, as those who benefit by providing profitable Services to the Beneficiaries of those transfer payments, must pay for their upkeep through taxation of their Profits. Tax incidences upon all only rises marginally, while the financing of the Fund Budgets becomes more sustainable.

The advantage to American Taxpayers comes with understanding of the levels of revenue which must be raised, to support Government Services and Programs. All Fund Budget contributions will have to be combined, and levels of those contributions can be evaluated. The total Economy must support all contributions, whether Special Fund Budgets, or General Revenues of Government. The integration of State and Local taxation in the form of Personal Exemptions treated as Business expense, uniting the entirety of Cost for all Government into one Package, allowing for total evaluation of the Cost. Americans can view the total Package, and possibly decide they could do with less Government; most certainly Government measures which favor the Few, at the cost and injury of the greatest majority.

The final impact will be for all, in the form of Sticker shock! A collated review of the total Tax assessment may entice even Politicians to stop excessive log-rolling; legislative practice where elected officials vote favorably on each other's Pork barrel projects. Special Interests will alter the focus, from seeking discriminatory favoritism for themselves, to forestalling excess spending which will increase their membership's tax burden. Ordinary Citizens will have greater understanding of what amount of their total income is being taken by their Government, and they will want a greater understanding of both the withdrawal process, and what it is used for. Proper Choice Economics will be served, as the assessed Tax rates will draw enlightened Public interest desiring full information.

Traditional Readers of this Author knows he often takes wide swings away from the initial subject, in order to provide background for further discussion. The Author now feels the Reader must get a greater grasp of the functioning Economy, before discussion can proceed. The Reader should be assured the discussion will return to Taxes, as soon as certain Economic precepts are advanced

SECTION II

Preface

The Author suffers increasing worries under the economic policy of the latter Bush administration. Economic Indicators fail to express vitality under the Supply-Side economic policy of the Administration. There has been a slow erosion of economic activity throughout the current Administration, with no real indication this erosion can be blamed on the events of September 11, or on the following Wars in Afghanistan and Iraq. Government debt, at all levels of Government, is beginning to accelerate rapidly as tax revenues fail. An increasing share of the remaining Tax revenues must be devoted to Debt service, a costly mechanism of little economic value to anyone. Tax Breaks designed to generate Investment fail, as Consumer Demand and Consumption deteriorate. The Economic forecast must be considered bleak.

Popular literature attempts to present glowing portraits on the Economy, attempts to buoy up what Consumer Demand and economic optimism which do exist. Economists cannot share the fairytale of the Public, as economic index numbers express systematic losses. Everyone tries to dismiss the growing Government debt, but confrontation must come; All must understand the growth of public debt comes not just from removal of Taxes, though it stands as the most horrifying component, but from loss of actual domestic production. This is a hemorrhage which must be addressed, before the Patient dies. This Productive loss has its Origin in depressed Consumer Demand and Consumption ratios leading to reduced Inventories, and hard capital, domestic investment not engaged in by Business; awaiting Consumer Demand and Consumption figures increases. The Literature attempts to propel Consumption, yet ignores the lack of funds in the hands of Consumers to accomplish the desired Purchase levels.

Monetarists insist it requires only extension of Credit, dismissing the necessity of Consumers to repay the contracted debt. Supply-Side Economists insist capital investment can spur Consumption, not differentiating between hard Capital construction and acquisition of financial instruments, avoiding the issue of Job growth. Tax Breaks provide only worsened Government deficit spending, without spurred Consumer Demand to excite Business investment. The current Administration deliberately avoids study of Marketing losses, where the absence of the Consumer is almost a national scandal; their participation suborned by

Tax Cuts and Mortgage refinancing under low Interest rates. They ignore the obvious, to avoid cancellation of Tax Breaks for the Corporate wealthy; probably the worst depressant among a long list of curtailments of Consumer Demand, as it maintains Corporate Pricing schedules. The nation moves forward, with an economic policy designed to destroy any economic factors favorable to Production. Economic success can come only with destruction of economic policy, which impedes economic performance.

Chapter I:
Introduction

Any Author on Economics will face an immense problem, practically from the start of his discussion. He has to make a judgement on the degree of training enjoyed by his Reader. A Reader of Economic text must start into the work, wondering if he has sufficient knowledge of the discussed Subject to render an evaluation. Economic Issues have become so complex; Professors of Economics cannot always be sure of comprehension, due to the vast expansion of Economic models and statistical material. This Author wishes to present coherent material for the basic Student, who may possess absolutely no prior organized knowledge of Economics. Everyone holds some intrinsic grasp of how Economics works through participation in the market of Goods and Services.

Everyone purchases Goods in the Economy. The Individual needs these Goods to establish and maintain his lifestyle. He purchases these Goods from a Producer, or from a Retailer who has purchased these Goods from a Producer, or from a Wholesaler who has purchased these Goods from a Producer for resale to Retailers. The Consumer, the Individual who purchases these Goods for his own consumption to maintain his lifestyle, uses Money to purchase Goods derived from his own position as Producer, Wholesaler, Retailer, or Financier of Production. He can be classified as an Employee or a Manager in any of the above Occupations, or he can be defined as an Owner of the Means of Production. It is quite clear the Economy is intrinsically focused on Production; every economic occupation purchases Goods gained from Production, and everyone pays for the Good by being involved with some process of Production. The only deviation from this basic format lie in purchase of Goods with Government welfare transfers, such determined by lack of participation in the Productive process. The element of Charity must all be considered, but Charity is only welfare transfer from private economic Participants given to non-Participants in the Productive process. The Reader can understand the importance of Production to both Economics and Consumers.

The Productive Process must also be examined, for it contains some very important elements which cannot be violated. It must be organized and financed. The Organization entails identification of the Product to be produced, the methodology with which the Product will be produced, and the resources which will be utilized in the Product's production. This process necessitates identification of Management, identification of Productive labor, the parameter of the Product and it's composition, and the technology used in Production. All of the Above remains the province of Management, coming from Entrepreneurs who make the decision to produce, this flowing from Individual choice or Government appointment. The need for finance appears immediately after the decision to produce, all following elements requiring payment for initiation of endeavor. Research and Design must be pay for, as they are Productive services provided by skilled Productive labor. The technology must be chosen and assembled; the scope selected by the designated design parameters of the Product. Productive labor must be hired and trained in the use of technology for production of the Product. Resources for both Training in Productive methods and actual Production need to be purchased and stored. This all must be accomplished before the actual production of the Product, though most comes only after a Test Product has been assembled in the Research stage.

Some Readers will insist there is no mention of the Service Industry in the above analysis, though there is. The Service industries are set up in almost exact format as is Production industry; Service industry's Product, though, consists of services to Consumers or Productive industry operation. Service Industry needs Management, Capitalization, Trained Labor force, and Productive equipment to produce their Services. They are simply a different form of Production industry, which provide aid to Consumers and Producers. Services can be as capitalized at the Telecommunications industry, or limited as Lawn Care Service for Office and Home.

Many Readers will think the previous analysis a simplistic outline without value, though beginning Students need such an outline, understanding the complexity of Economics starts with simple statements, where the Student gains comprehension of the totality. A study outline of Productive finance may introduce greater interest for those educated in the Economic process. It is sufficient to state Productive finance must also be financially capitalized, this through derivation of Profits from Production. Productive finance also requires several elements which must be served.

The Productive financier has to first find a source of funds. These funds must come from some previous involvement within the Productive process of the

Economy; whether they are previous Wages, Profits, or borrowed funds from financial instruments; most Productive funds coming from the latter source. Profits from Production provide return to Productive finance, no matter which original source is utilized, and Production cannot be maintained, if these Profits fail to materialize. The only alteration from this structure comes as Government underwriting of unprofitable Production to serve Government interest, another form of welfare transfer, and One which swells to the most expensive form of welfare transfer—both to the Taxpayer and the Economy.

There are a number of constituent elements necessary to provide profitability to a Product. The Product must hold economic value to some Consumer; i.e., it must provide some establishment or maintenance of the lifestyle for the Individual purchasing, else he will not purchase the Product. The Product has to serve some economic value first of all. It must withstand competition in the Market for such Goods, so that it must be the superior or equal in value to any other Product, the only variant to this necessity being much lower Product cost, without losing a substantial amount of value in use for the Consumer. Productive cost of the Product must be sufficiently low as Profits can be attained, with sale of Product at competitive price in the Market. The largesse of this Productive Profit is in itself important; it must be of size sufficient to provide adequate Return to the amount of Capitalization used, in both the Organizational and Productive process. Insufficient Productive profit will lead to under-funding of the Productive effort, and Production will eventually cease.

Technology becomes paramount in the Productive Process for a number of reasons. Technology remains the source for efficient Production in the first place. It is the avenue for cutting the cost of Production, by utilization of cheaper amounts of Resource, and reduced amounts of Labor and Capital. It is also the greatest threat to Productive Profits, due to the fact it remains the true venue for competition between Products in the Marketplace. This Threat is not minor, as can be seen by the development of Patent Law; the process where technological advantage is protected in the Marketplace. Technology, though, also has serious Costs, mainly in the form of Labor retraining costs, and more expensive Capitalization of Production.

The matrix is completed with the process of Marketing. This consists of the formula for getting Consumer awareness of the availability of the Product. Production generates no sale of Product, if the Consumer does not know of the existence of the Product. It requires Distribution of Product, so the Product arrives at an arena where Consumers can purchase, a costly effort to maintain in itself, often needing a network of Retail outlets and Service venues. It continues to the area of Advertising, where Product identification and availability are brought to media attention and the Consumer. The area of Marketing in total has been growing as an element of Production Costs, though has been showing some signs of abatement in later years. Reasons for this consist in the multiplicity of Products available with high degree of Trade substitution, with little ability to promote long-term Brand loyalty; the rising cost of Advertising within a spectrum of overuse of advertisements; and the need to maintain Product unit Profitability. Advertising saturation concepts have changed; with almost no ability to dominant a Product market; altering the emphasis to Product durability and function, from an earlier attempted establishment of Brand loyalty among Consumers.

The Production cycle can be seen as a complex function, traveling from Entrepreneurial idea, then Research and Design, to Investor and Hard Capitalization, training Labor, Production itself, establishment of distribution networks, and training of Retail labor plus Advertising. Many Steps of the process can be averted, but most only at the cost of long-term Profitability. The importance of this interlocking network lies in the fact all must be adequately complete, before the Return on Investment can be attained. Production Profits must be realized if the real goal of Production is attained: the enrichment of the Producers. The Author here states the Reader should not express any contempt for the Producers; no one functions in the Economy, either as Producer or Consumer, without this enrichment for themselves; it is the means they utilize to be Economic participants.

Difficulty enters the equation at this point because of the natural construct of the Economic Consumer. He is a mythical creature which does not actually exist, there being such a vast diversity in economic tastes. The Economist, though, will explain the Consumer can be quantified, so that a statistical model of the average Consumer can be constructed. Some incredible numbers of characteristics can be assigned to this mythical Consumer: average Income, standard of living, preferred colors, preferred types of packaging, most desired products as determined by Disposable dollars designated for product purchase, degree of knowledge held on product availability, order of preference in purchasing decisions, and amount of purchases to be made in any Time period. The difficulty described above comes in the fact the above information is highly volatile, with wide flux on purchasing decisions due to economic pressures placed on the Consumer.

The Consumer reacts almost instantly to alterations in Income, thinking to expand or contract his purchases based not only on his immediate income, but also on estimates of possible effects on his future income. This adjustment occurs at the point of potential purchase of Product (i.e., at the Retailers). Later discussions will delineate the concepts of Disposable Income, Projected Earnings, Incremental Income Allotments, and Averaged Irreducible Expenses. It is sufficient here to explain that even temporary shortages of consistent Income will lead to immediate change in Consumption patterns, and even the threat of such shortages will lead to such alteration. Expectation of higher Income will lead to expenditure patterns pushing to increase of purchases, which cannot be sustained under circumstances where Income remains unchanged, leading to an overall reduction of Consumption, in order to fund the excessive prior purchase decisions. There is the case of the Individual who bought a Cadillac under expectation of a Promotion, only to fail in the Promotion and continuing life on a Chevy budget. A more relevant case is an Individual who purchased a new car because of added Income from working Overtime hours, only to revert to a normal Workweek.

The Consumer possesses many other bad characteristics for both Economist and Businessman. Most mechanics cannot name more than 20 percent of the new model cars available for sale in his area; less knowledgeable Consumers can hardly find the car model suitable to his needs, with Dealer and Salesmen little aid in advising on models which they do not sell. Most Consumers know three times as much about automobiles, than they do about Housing, and know far less about Electronics than either. Discount Retail houses compete on the basis of Product prices, with almost no attempt to explain function. The only educational process available for most Consumers comes in the form of Advertising, not noted for clarity of Product function. Business finds this ignorance profitable; the Economist finds it deplorable, knowing at least half of all Consumers could be served better with alternate Products, often of cheaper price. Product comparison magazines fill part of the gap, but suffer from dishonesty of service in examination of Advertising Products, and fail in Readership due to Consumer inattention after immediate purchase decisions are made.

Current political leadership is basically Business-oriented to the point most Consumer Safeguard agencies are left unfunded. The actual threat to the Consumer remains minor, but the long-term cost is lack of Product comparison venues. Some Economic studies have been conducted, to attempt to quantify the economic losses occasioned from the lack of Product comparison. The Author evaluates that purchase of unsuitable Product costs almost 2 percent of Total Consumption dollars in this Country; he does know he is the new Owner of a Pick-up truck build for heavy transportation while he mainly uses it for intercity commutes, the wrong choice probably costing a loss of Ten miles per gallon of gas. He bought it new from a Dealer salesman, who informed him it was just what he needed. He is sure he is not the only Consuming Fool in America.

Another factor enjoyed by Business, but detested by the Economist, came in the fact almost all Consumers are Plunge buyers. Interesting products will be purchased upon discovery, creating imbalances in Consumer budgets; this imbalance often leading to a Consumer debt ratio some 30 percent higher than need be, causing Interest charges which distract from a larger Consumption pattern. This may seem like a picayune observation, until it is stated as probable loss of 4 percent of total potential Consumption. Many Product/Labor Studies have been conducted, but One can be sure this Shortfall causes the equivalent of fifty thousand jobs in the Economy. Public school classes teaching adequate Consumption procedures could possibly cut this loss in half, though loss of Buying skill would be rapid as the classes receded into Student memory.

The Consumer lacks an overall evaluation of his financial position. No organization stipulates a detailed Household scenario based upon Income levels. Every Consumer lacks clear identification of economic status, almost totally defined by Bank extension of mortgages. The relaxation of Bank procedures for such extension, leaves this definition almost without validity. The Consumer, today, finds declining Mutual Fund values, very low Interest rates on financial instruments, inability of fund aggregation for individual investment, and constant consistent values only in residential properties. The Consumer is overinvested in Housing as consequence, all based upon large mortgages which deny expansion of other forms of Consumer credit. Several Economic studies express widely divergent estimates of the damage, but the Author believes overcapitalization of residential properties incite at least a 9 percent loss of Consumer Demand. This being due not to mortgage rates, which are low, but due to the loss of Consumer credit extension and absorbed Discretionary Income paying excessive mortgage service.

An important element of the above discussion affects Construction Cost scheduling extensively. The high consistent real estate values pressures for construction of high resale value properties. Normal Working Class housing has been abandoned, replaced with moderate wealth estates construction. Economic studies indicate such foci of construction have increased rental rates by 30 percent above projected Normal, pressured Working Class families to devote another 20 percent of their Discretionary Income to housing, and have expanded the number of families without Housing by a factor of Three. It has also expanded the period of a resale from Three months to Two years; this process incurring listing charges and lengthy payments of property necessities—like heating, property tax, and mortgage payments. The higher Property values of construction have also forced up the cost of purchase of empty lots for construction; when combined by a refusal of construction in older urban areas, has made these increases probably the greatest in the Economy. Consolidation of all these Economic factors into some statistical model remains almost impossible, though the Author estimates such expanded expenses produce a 17–20 percent decrease in Consumer Demand.

The Consumer also faces Corporate Product Price schedules. These schedules set Product prices at levels which produce economic profits for the Corporation, through which they can aggregate financial assets rapidly. These economic profits produce wicked Product price increases. Most Automobile companies finance their extension of Consumer credit solely through these excess Product prices, meaning Consumers pay both for the Product, and for the extension of credit through higher Product prices. Continual price increases come not from increased cost of Product manufacture, which have actually decreased, but need of greater funds for credit extension. Extension of Corporate Consumer Credit rather than normal financial institution credit probably doubles the cost to the Consumer, in terms of total overall Interest payments. The individual Consumer can do little about this, as most of the increases are reflected in Product price initial cost, this product price setting the largesse of the initial loan. This process can be estimated to cost a loss of 15 percent of Consumer Demand—through higher Product prices and Interest charges.

The Reader can quickly determine the Author fears current economic structure, due to its impact upon Consumer Demand. This term remains vital to the Economist, who know it means Consumers with money in their pockets—either as Cash or Credit cards, with willingness to purchase at current prices. The current economic structure is draining Consumer Demand from the system. Improvement does not call for alteration of procedure, just amendment of the procedures of Government and Business. A Free Market system remains the most positive force to increase economic performance, and increase the Standard of Living of all. The necessity, in fact, lies in reintroduction of free market forces into the current system, forces which Government and Business procedures have diminished in impact and effect. Much of the following material will be devoted to removing what the Author calls the bureaucratization of the free enterprise system.

Chapter II:
Definition of Consumer Demand

Consumer Demand stands as a simple concept: The aggregate desire for Goods and Services expressed by all Consumers in the Economy. All includes Business elements and Government in the matrix, not just End-Consumers of these Goods and Services. Business competes with private Consumers through the process of Investment and Resource Demand. Older Economic analysis equated hard capital investment to a direct reduction of private End-Consumption. Current Economic analysis has developed several theories which modify the older analysis, insisting reductions of Investment actually decreases End-Consumption Demand. This modification has proven to be statistically accurate. Capital equipment and facilities provision Sectors are high-Wage Sectors generating greater Consumer Demand, than is diminished by Investment through loss of Income by reduction of Profits distribution, Interest payments, and higher Goods pricing. Government duplicates private Consumption by purchase of Goods and Services for welfare programs, and imitates Business investment by entering into Infrastructure construction.

The essential elements to Consumer Demand consist of desire for Consumption, with the second condition of ability to pay for that Consumption. The desire for Consumption must contain the willingness to consume at the Prices demanded for that Consumption, this establishing the Price schedule for Goods and Services. The willingness to consume diminishes as the Price of such Consumption increases. This willingness increases as Price reduces. Everyone would like to drive a Cadillac or Porsche, but Few are those willing to detail such a amount of their total income for the provision of personal transportation. Most are willing to accept a cheaper substitution, even though Consumption satisfaction may not be as great. This presents a fundamental economic theory of Economics: Consumers will transfer to more unsatisfactory substitute Goods and Services with increases in Pricing.

This Principle need be examined in greater detail. Willingness to consume at a specific Price can be designated as the desire to allocate a certain net percentage of

Consumer Income for the specific Good or Service. This is a personal desire on the part of the Consumer, and can be generated by many motives. The allocation procedure, though, remains highly dependent on the Economic factors of largesse of Income, or ability to fund Consumption by borrowing, also finally dependent upon the largesse of Income. It is also highly dependent upon the Consumer's perception of the state of his total Income. This view is not wholly chaotic, as many Laymen and some Economists insist. It consists of many parts: the Consumer's expectation of increase or decrease of total Income, his belief of Product pricing increasing or decreasing as percentage element of his total Income, and his belief that unavoidable Expenses is increasing or decreasing net percentage of his total Income. The actual alteration of Product pricing and Expense affects the first factor of Consumer willingness, while the more subjective second factor is deeply influenced by Public perception of the state of the total Economy. Business practice fears the power of the second evaluative process, using various add-on charges to make a profit; without a statement of the total Product cost, until the Consumer is committed to Product purchase.

Switch to more expensive Goods and Services is much less rapid than is the process of transfer to cheaper substitute Goods and Services. The basic rationale for this statistically proven fact derives from the ability to switch to more expensive Products; it stays almost completely dependent upon an actual increase of total Income or ability to borrow for Consumption; still innately tied to limits of total Income. Switch to cheaper Goods and Services is not dependent on actual increase or decrease of total Income, simply on perceptions of potential alteration of total Income. The former switch actually lags behind increases in total Income, with some period of delay. The latter switch often proceeds actual decreases in total Income, and may even occur where there is no decrease in total Income, possibly even in the presence of total Income increases.

The Banker worries about actual changes in total Income, as does the Consumer; the Economist must worry about Consumer perceptions of the Economy and it's performance. Actual statistics indicate Consumer Demand of the individual Consumer will lag Eleven months behind actual net increases of total Income, in that average Consumer Demand for each specific Income level will not be reached for that period of time. This Consumer Demand only rises to the Income level average with expectation that the net increase will be maintained. The period time lag can be lengthened to forty-eight months, if this expectation does not exist. A perceived threat of decrease of total Income can proceed actual reduction of Income by Four months, and can continue for forty-eight months without any actual reduction of total Income. Such is the power of Consumer perception of adverse effect on their Income levels.

Economic examination of these conditions brings depression to both Economist and Businessman. Economic performance insists on high, consistent Consumer Demand. Several Economic studies express clearly there must be a switch to more expensive Goods and Services by Consumers, in order to maintain an Economic Boom past Twenty months. It has already been indicated there is an eleven-month lag behind actual total Income increases, before this switch will normally occur. This lag will be lengthened, if Consumer perceptions doubt actual maintenance of total Income increases. The Businessman and Economist must convince Consumers of continued good economic performance within Twenty months, or an Economic Boom will not be maintained. They have to convince Consumers that life is getting better, and is going to stay that way for a considerable period of time.

The reciprocal also expresses itself adversely. Consumers will switch to cheaper substitute Goods and Services at signs of poor Economic performance, which could impact their lifestyle badly. The major factors which incite such a switch remain a threat of total Income loss through Layoffs or loss of Overtime, increased unavoidable Expenses, increased Interest rates on Consumer credit, Product price increases, and Business suppression of Wage increases. The Student must remember a Consumer will switch to a cheaper substitute prior to a total Income loss, and will not switch to more expensive Product until proven total Income increases have been in place for about Eleven months. The perception of the Consumer, therefore, is the actual determinant of Boom and Bust cycles. An Economic Boom can only be maintained for Twenty months, without a switch to more expensive Products by Consumers. Such a Boom will be killed within Three months of a switch to cheaper substitute Products. The turnaround time from Economic Bust to Boom requires Eleven to Fifteen months, if the Consumers believe their lifestyle is improving, due to the lag of a switch to more expensive Product behind net increases in total Income.

Government, Business, and the Economist cannot hide actual economic statistics from the Consumers. They will react in a negative manner, if poor economic performance is indicated, with a potential switch to cheaper substitute Products. Advertising, or Propaganda campaigns, will not work effectively to dissuade Consumers from this negative behavior, if adverse economic conditions continue for longer than Three months. Government, Business, and Economist must counteract adverse economic conditions within Ten months of their inception, else favorable economic conditions will be destroyed, with the Economy entering into a Recession. The Economist can only advise Government and Business; whose actions are necessary to forestall those adverse economic conditions, before a Recession occurs.

The Government infects Consumer expectations of future Personal Income in a multitude of ways, and so impact Consumer Demand drastically, most of the impact being adverse in nature. Higher taxation means lowered Disposable Income for Consumers, with an impact on Consumer Demand greater than the total tax withdrawal from Consumers. Greater Government expenditures engender increased competition with private Consumers in sought Goods and Services. This includes not only the actual purchases, but also the increased Consumer Demand created by Payrolls paid to Employees for production of Government products. Actual Economic evolution through the Production process indicates an actual decrease of Goods and Services to private Consumption, where Government purchases actually exceed 18 percent of GDP, when Unemployment is less than 8 percent. The Author admits this is a highly controversial Economic study, denied by almost all except for himself.

The connotations of such an actual decrease of Goods and Services available to private Consumption hold vast detriment for the Economy. The actual shortfall may vary between 8–16 percent of the total value of Government purchases within the Economy above 14.3% of GDP. The latter figure is called a lateral breakeven point, so stipulated as a null point where Government economic action holds no enjoined economic impact. Less Government spending than this Point would lead to a drop of Production, Government expenditure past this Point incites pressures on Resource prices, Wage levels, and Consumption patterns. This establishes that a expenditure pattern by Government less than 14.3% of GDP brings a loss of total GDP. An expenditure pattern by Government above 14.3% of GDP also brings some degree of loss of total GDP, due to Inflationary pressures. The Outcome of the Analysis resembles Limit theory in Calculus, with the value of 14.3% of Gross Domestic Product as limit; percentage variances from the limit impacting percentage differences in GDP.

The total levels of Government expenditure in this Country—at all three levels—has long exceeded 14.3% of GDP. The Inflationary pressures produced by this expenditure pattern can be minimized or maximized. The greatest avenue of minimization of Inflationary pressures by such expenditure comes through high taxation, which fully underwrites Government expenditures, leading to direct reduction in Consumer Demand equal to loss of Product. Some Economists would deny complete reduction of Consumer Demand, due to the increased Consumer Demand engendered by Wages paid for Government Products. This

Author stipulates the high taxation falls equally upon all Wages, with Government-derived Wages equally taxed. The Inflationary pressure by Tax-funded Government expenditures in excess of 14.3% of GDP can be estimated to be less than .3% of the expenditure levels above 14.3% of GDP.

The worst avenue which brings the highest Inflationary pressures lay in a refusal of Government to fund its expenditures. Inflationary pressures grow exponentially. Private Consumer Demand is not reduced by taxation. Greater Consumer Demand is created by Interest charge increases due to the added demand for Funds, and Wage payments for Government production. Production is actually decreased by the increased Operating Costs; a minimum equal to or greater than added Interest charges paid for financial Capital. Wages increases are suppressed by increased Consumer Product prices, while a greater Work load is demanded; leading to increased Wage and Work benefits demands. The Worker benefits increase Business Cost, as the guaranteed provision becomes more expensive to Insurers; this incited by reduced Production for Private Consumption. Wage payments for Government Goods and Services remain untaxed higher than Wages from private Consumer Production, so Consumer Demand is increased in direct proportion to the after-tax Wages paid for Government-sponsored Production.

The above analysis must be admitted as particularly the Author's own, with few if any Economists in total agreement. All regularly state there exist mitigating circumstances of economic magnitude, which cancels out the economic impact of the above forces. None are forthcoming about the exact nature of those mitigating circumstances. The Author states here effective Economic argument has not been presented to counteract the above economic analysis, and study of Economic statistics express full generation of the Inflationary pressures indicated. Consumer Demand is only beneficial, if and only if it does not generate excessive Inflationary pressures. The greatest Inflationary pressure from Consumer Demand comes in the form of unfunded Government expenditure.

A short detour must be made to examination of Inflation and Inflationary pressures. Inflation is nothing more than an increase of Product prices, which is generated by Inflationary pressures. These express themselves in a multiplex of ways, and Economists have extreme difficulty in defining them exactly. Classical Economists simply accepted the element of Inflation, and discounted the causes for it; stating these Inflationary pressures were the product of increased Economic activity and Production—a factor of Economic growth. Later Economists accounted Inflation to be the result of increased Resource Demand, concurrent with increased Cost of technology. Current Economists believe Inflation results from a lack of financial liquidity, alongside increased Distribution Costs from increased volumes distributed.

The Author denies all of the above Arguments for Inflation generation. None of the Arguments accept the averaging of Costs throughout the Economy, so increases in Production volume actually do not produce increased Costs; except in the Resource market, these reduced in Cost by equivalent Technological inputs with the rest of the Economy, so there would be no Inflationary pressure generated. The impact of Costs is still averaged throughout the Economy, the Blend producing no inflationary pressure. This averaging of total Economic Costs nullifies any Inflationary pressures generated by Technological Cost increases. The inflationary pressure on Resource pricing equals only the added Wage payments for technological inputs, the capital cost being averaged in the total Capital/Profits spectrum without inflationary effect.

The Author believes Inflationary pressures generate only by under-funding of the Production process. His first stipulation states it does not mean Inflation is generated by Interest rates on borrowed Capital. Interest charges on borrowed Capital remain a normal Production Cost, and elimination of such Charges would actually reduce Production levels, reduce Consumer Demand, and actually incite Inflationary pressures, the result of abnormal stress in the Production schedule. Production schedules operate normally with borrowed Funds; failure of these Funds can only detract from the Production cycle. Economic studies conducted, have expressed loss of Production due solely to reliance on aggregated Capital (Savings); the process slowed technological innovation, normal expansions of Production levels, and lower Profit levels due to artificial Recapitalization rates.

Under-Funding of the Production process is not a reduced Funding of the total Production process. Averaging of Production Costs through the total Economy insists that each Production process be fully-funded. The Author's thesis specifically states such under-Funding restrict solely within each of the Sectors of Production. The total Production process must be fully-funded due to the averaging of Cost in the total Economy; so return from other Sectors of Production must be increased, to make up for shortfalls in Funding by any one Sector. The under-Funding of one or more Sectors means Cost increases in the other Sectors of Production, as these Sectors must accept Product delivery delays, or assumed alterations of resource from the underfunded Supplier. This increase is Inflationary pressure, as it means economic Profits for the underfunded Sectors, and reduced entrepreneurial Profits for all other Sectors of Production. The underfunded Sectors incite excessive Consumer Demand due to their economic profits, while the remaining Sectors produce less Product but with static provision of Consumer Demand. Consumer Demand rises in relationship to levels of Production, only acceptable if the underfunded Sectors use the economic profits to fund their Production activities. Here is the specific arena where Inflation is generated. It must be admitted other Economists do not accept this Argument.

> [The Author has received criticism for the above paragraph, it making claim as either being confusing, or saying nothing. Underfunded Sectors of Production do not supply Resource in the form desired, or do so only after Production delivery delays. Receiving Sectors of Production must accept the delayed delivery schedule as loss of Production. They must also input capital equipment and work scheduling to alter resource received into proper utilization form. The added-Costs reduce their Profits, with lowered rates of Production. The economic Profits derived by underfunded Sectors translates as increased Consumer demand—whether of Production capital or Wage increases to Labor in the Sector. Wage rates are relatively stable in all Sectors, so the Production losses mean actual increased Consumer Demand in all Sectors, due to the delayed length of Production time. It resolves into lowered Production schedules coupled to increased Consumer Demand, i.e., inflationary pressure leading to Inflation.

The principle of Production Cost averaging in the total Economy must be explored for the understanding of the Student. The Averaging occurs through the process of all Goods and Services in the Economy being in competition with each other for every Consumption dollar. Consumer Demand alters through Price competition between these Products. The Process does not simply dictate how much of each Product is consumed. It also determines the rates of return for the Production process; setting the Profit ratios, Wage levels, acceptable Interest charges to be paid, and the amount of total technological capitalization utilized. All are set by the rate of return given to each element in the Production process. The prices for the various Products determine the amount of total Investment in Production which each Product will have. The final outcome determines a repayment schedule for each element of Production; with the usage of the various elements limited or expanded because of the largesse of the repayment. It works out to an Average Wage paid for each hour worked, differentiated only by increments of Education, Training, and Technological equipment used; so there is a uniform value to Money itself: a Dollar equaling a Dollar. It is the same for Capital, Technological Equipment, Operating Capital, Resource prices, and even Taxation. It establishes a consistent price to Money, all based upon the Production Schedules for Goods and Services, at the same time setting the quantity of any Product which will be produced at any given Price for that Product.

Inflationary pressure is generated when there are artificial structures created within the operating cycle of total Production, which precludes this averaging process. Inflation is actually realized, if these structures can overcome the Averaging aspects of the total Economy, so other factors of Production must pay in less return for the above-average return of the specific Sectors protected by adamant Price structures. All Return schedules are altered, and Production is reduced in Product areas which cannot resist the added Cost to Production. This forces a Product price rise due to contraction of the quantity of Product supplied. Impediments to the Averaging process often raise their own Return at this point, propelling another round of unequal Return. This Process of Inflation will continue until the blocking structures to Averaging have been overborne by reduced Consumer Demand for the protected-Price Products. This is the total Generator of Inflation in the Long-run, and 80 percent of Inflation in the Short-run.

Economic studies indicate added Costs of Production due to Resource Cost increases, increased Consumer Demand, Technological Cost increases, and Acts of God will not increase Product prices in the Long-run, due to the Averaging process. All such Expenses spread throughout the Economy, and the added Cost reduces to normal Production figures, this true even for heavily-capitalized Technological advances. The critical factor here in the reduction comes in the number of Participants in the new Production schedule for the Product in question. The added Cost is normalized by the Fifth or Sixth Generations of Sales of the Product, the result of Participant spread in the added Production Cost schedule. The Dollar equals a Dollar averaging has returned to its original position.

Government expenditure above 14.3% of GDP without fully-funding the expenditure creates an artificial structure of image Employment, whose Wages are borrowed. It also creates the same image Capitalization, and image Profits, image Interest payments, image Production. The word 'image' is used in the Economic sense alone, where Production Costs remain unpaid, though the Production process can continue with the use of the image. The End-result equates to lessened total Production because of high Product prices with increased Consumer cost, expansion of the Money Supply to pay for the increased Pricing, and a total reduction of the Profits from Production. This is all conducted under the Scenario that Taxpayers are committed to the final payment for the Image, along with Debt Service charges.

The serious Student should understand the figure 14.3% of GDP for Government expenditures is, in itself, highly controversial. Classical, Neo-Classical, Supply-Side Economists, and Monetarists all basically disagree, stating Government identifies exactly with a normal private Consumer. They ignore completely the largesse of Government; the stated figure still leaves Government the largest Employer, largest Purchaser, and largest Contractor by a multiple of some hundreds. They refuse to accept deficit spending makes Government the largest User of Consumer Credit in existence, massively multiplying the amount of Credit extension. They deny extended use of Deficit spending by Government equates with the largest Enterprise in the World refusing to pay its Operating Expenses. The figure cited, 14.3%, represents the amount of Government expenditure allowed before it impedes normal utilization of Resources by Private Sector enterprise. A lesser Government expenditure leads to lack of exploitation of Resource, as greater Government expenditure leads to contraction of the Private Sector exploitation of Resource—materials, Labor, and Technological Capitalization. Remember this statistical data works only with an Unemployment rate of less than 8 percent; higher Unemployment highlights underutilization of Resources and Productive capacity.

The Above expresses clearly that Americans pay, or don't pay, for too many Government Goods and Services. It is a detriment to maintaining a Full Employment of the Economy. The most important economic initiative would be to fully-fund Government expenditures by taxation, which reduces the Inflationary pressures of Government expenditure. It would place Government in an equivalent position with Private Industry, where Expenses bring a reduction to Consumer Demand. An Economic study suggests increases of GDP by such action could repay the loss by Government Contract reductions within Three years. Phasing out excessive Government expenditures could actually increase GDP faster than Employment losses from reduced Government spending. Most of this Section will be an examination of various alteration to Government expenditure patterns, along with alteration of various Business practices which is not conducive to economic performance.

Chapter III:
Gross Domestic Product

This quantum series of Statistical evaluation is a highly versatile tool helping Economists in understanding economic performance as a Whole. It also possesses numerous shortcomings, as it presents little statistical detail of the interior activity of the Production process. The interior funding of the Production cycle lacks declaration in functional total. The GDP as it is commonly known, therefore, most particularly detracts rather than enlightens; when Tax policy is to be reviewed and discussed. Almost all current Economic thought tends to believe the interior funding within the Production cycle should be left untaxed, for the singular purpose of economic efficiency. The Author sharply disagrees with this assessment, and will explain this dispute later in this Work. It is sufficient here to state the GDP does not mark the financial flow of funding through the Production process at all. The GDP simply produces gross monetary magnitudes for the Goods and Services produced in the Economy.

The Production cycle consists of many intervening steps, which a current segment of Economists like to assign the name 'added value'; doing so because they believe an equitable tax can be assigned to these increments of value. The Author here disagrees as will be explained later, but the importance to the discussion lies in the fact every intervening step requires a financial payment at the specific point, in order for the step to be accomplished. The totality of payments at these intervening steps is called the Financial Flow of the Production Cycle. This Flow has many ramifications to Economics, most notably the speed of Funds into the Cycle, the speed of payment in the Cycle, and the speed of reentry of Funds into the Cycle by Consumer Demand.

The direction of Funds into the Cycle initially is called Capitalization of Production. Monetarist Economic theory concentrates on this Capitalization, and maintenance of Consumer Demand for establishing the financial instruments for this Funding. Consumer Demand must eventually fund this Capitalization through purchase of the Products of Production. It does this by purchasing the Products of Production, paying for the Production cycle with the addition of

Profits for that Production. These Profits from Production are what generates the financial instruments to fund future Production. The Monetarists basically stop their analysis at the point of providing Capitalization to the Production process. It remains the basic shortcoming of their theory, as they fail to undertake study of the rest of the Financial Flow of the Production Cycle.

The speed of payment for the intervening steps in the Cycle holds equal weight with the considerations of the Monetarists. Greater rapidity of payment reduces the cost of Operating Capital for Recipients of step payments, allowing for lower Product provision cost to the greater Production cycle. Receipt of Payment turns the Receiver into a Consumer, as he undertakes to buy Goods and Services, both for his own Consumption as End-Consumer, and in production of further Product to provide to the greater Production cycle. The speed of payment with the Cycle, therefore, determines the immediate cost of intervening Steps of Production, and development of further Capitalization for Production. A slower speed of intervening Step payment means a higher cost of Step provision, with greater capitalization for that Step. Faster speed of intervening Step payment lower cost of step provision, with less Capitalization for that Step. This may not seem of importance to the Layman, but variances of 34% of intervening Step cost can be observed, along with a 40% differential in observed Capitalization of the intervening Step. The Author estimates the speed of payment of intervening Steps in the Production cycle can expand or contract total Capitalization for Production in the Economy by as much as 20 percent of total Capitalization.

The reentry of Funds into the Production cycle requires Consumption of the Products produced, which is dependent upon Consumer Demand. A strengthening of Consumer Demand means an increase in speed of reentry of Funds, and a softening of Consumer Demand means a slowing of reentry of Funds into the Production cycle. The former actually translates into an increase of Capitalization for Production, with enhanced economic growth for the Economy, the latter meaning a reduction of Capitalization with lessened or no economic growth. Economic studies are beginning to compile statistical evidence that Businessmen will not invest in capital equipment to increase Production, when there is a softening of Consumer Demand, no matter the level of potential capitalization. This states they will not undergo the financial risk of adding Productive equipment, when there is insufficient observed Consumer Demand for more Product; this observance expressed in draft of Inventories. This observance is highly resistant to lowered Costs of Capitalization, so lowered Interest rates will not provide incentive to business investment in Productive capitalization with witnessed soft Consumer Demand for Product. The relevant element delaying Business investment resides in the lengthened duration of Production Step payments, due to the soft Consumer Demand expressed. The Author interjects this analysis here, as refutation of current Economic policy by Federal Reserve and Government, which concentrates upon ease of Capitalization rather than a systematic program to increase Consumer Demand.

Return to the Production Cycle requires further study of the Process. Payment for intervening Steps in the Production cycle turns the Recipients into Consumers, as they purchase Goods and Services. This is a highly important Economic factor! It proclaims Capital aggregation by reentry of funds into the Production cycle does not await completion of the Production cycle, just completion of intervening Steps of Production. Only payment for the initial Capitalization of Production awaits final End-Consumption of Product. Here is found the real divergence between potential Capitalization and Business willingness to invest. Business investment awaits payment for the initial Capitalization of Production, which is dependent on sufficient Consumer Demand. Capital aggregation awaits only payment of intervening Step costs of Production. Economic policy to spur Capital aggregation is irrelevant, as it is spurred by payment of the intervening Step costs of Production. Willingness to invest is dependent on final payment of Production capitalization through Consumption. There is always Capital aggregation sufficient for Business investment. Consumer Demand for Product is necessary to incite such Business investment. Current Economic policy puts the carts before the horse. It is Consumer Demand which generates Business investment, not Capital aggregation through Production Profits, a function which is natural to the Production process.

Tax Policy, because of the above conditions, needs to concentrate on maximization of Consumer Demand, not on provision of opportunity for capital aggregation. Study of Tax Policy expresses a strong enmity between the Two, with measures taken individually to maximize capital aggregation inhibiting Consumer Demand, and vice versa. Tax measure which eases the fulfillment of One, generally curtails the Other to some degree. A Case in point comes in the shift of Consumption Debt from Consumer Credit to Mortgages over the last two decades, because of the freedom of deduction of Mortgage expense. Most Economists extol the merits of the Construction Boom incited, but Clothing and Non-Durable Goods have suffered a 20 percent loss of total Consumption Debt causation. This translates at almost a 30 percent loss of their market, with almost a 60 percent loss of Profitability for Retail stores. Homeowners surveyed possesses aged Clothing, fewer Non-Durable Goods, and average 40 percent less furniture and Appliances than two decades' previous. The amount of these Goods which have been obtained under Sales conditions has tripled, a very serious source of loss of Profitability to Retailers.

An interesting note on the Tax Policy emphasis on Savings comes in the form that American workers are working longer hours, with higher Debt/Savings ratios, and are buying less Product. Economists insist this is a good directional effort, because there will be a higher Capital/Maintenance ratio later in life. This does not account for the higher expenditure in Debt Service, the increasing cost of Product in order to fund the greater financial capitalization of the Production cycle with less actual Sale of Product, and the lack of in-depth accumulation of Consumption products. Most indications express a lower Standard of Living based on expensive Consumer products, coupled with over-expensive Housing with heightened Maintenance costs, and no easy Sale of Housing within limits of normal return to Capitalization. There was an old expression declaring Ranchers to be Grass-Poor; a new expression could be Consumers who are the two-by-four Proud.

The Reader probably asks by this time, what does this Information have to do with the Gross Domestic Product. The answer is that it determines the makeup of the Gross Domestic Product. The Construction industry has led the Economy for decades, determining there is excessive actual Square feet of Building. This can be said in the face of the fact that Housing is mainly missing for the Poor and Working Poor. The ratio of New/Used Housing Prices is too high, and the price of Used Housing remains 40 percent overpriced. Rental rates are excessive, reflective of the overlarge Mortgage payments. The Period of Sale for Housing has lengthened dramatically with the increased Pricing, with the Poor and Working Poor priced out of the Market. It is estimated by the Author that most of the Working Poor could be housed adequately in the empty Housing units, which Rental and Sales agents refuse allowance to devalue them. These Individuals and the Owners would rather keep them empty, and defray the loss from their taxes as Operating losses. The Housing shortage remains acute in the face of overbuilding.

Utilities continue to raise their rates in the face of falling Consumption of their services, because Price suppression of their Product has been disallowed, alongside reduction of taxation of their Profits. The outcome is rather humorous, being failure of Service during periods of Peak consumption. It is all conducted inside a milieu of increasing Capitalization Costs, because of Construction expansion. Maintenance problems are increasing, while Service personnel is declining. The practice of passing overt Fuel costs over to the Consumer worsens the situation, as Consumers are forced to pay higher rates for less service; with new constructions being the major source of Utilities cost increases. Already strapped Consumer Demand is burdened with additional set costs, not under Consumer control, while Consumer use of Utility services has become highly conscious and efficient. The only effective counter to this effect comes in the form of forcing new Constructions to fully fund Service provision, something which would triple the costs of Service connection. Current Government regulation and Contractor pressure forestalls this avenue: a new Homeowner does not want to pay Twenty Thousand Dollars for Service hookup.

Almost all large Corporations have entered the arena of Consumer Credit provision. They underwrite their Customers' purchases themselves, but aided by lack of Government regulation as are supervising Competitor Banks and S&Ls, and tax allowance as claimed investment. This seems like a wondrous idea, vastly increasing Consumer purchases for their Products, most Economists lauding the advance. Serious hazards are innate to the Process. Corporations escape taxation of their Profits, which are diverted to finance Consumer Credit to their Customers. They can offer lower Interest charges allowable to their financial institution counterparts. Customers still need financial institutions for their normal conduct in the Economy—a place to house their interim cash. Customers find themselves overextended in Consumer credit, because the emphasis of the Corporations is pushing Product, not the economic viability of the Customers. Customers find themselves with higher Credit payments, higher charges at their financial institutions who charge more for services to make up lost Profits, and increased taxation. The net result becomes loss of Consumer Demand, evaporated in Interest charges, higher Prices, and greater taxation.

Tax Policy has altered the nature of Business, and therefore, the mix of Gross Domestic Product. The diversion of taxation through Investment has increased the level of financial commitment, while actually inhibiting Consumer Demand, as Funds are diverted to Investment to escape taxation. The entirety of Upper-level Incomes is constricting their already restricted Consumption, as means of tax evasion. The increased levels of financial assets insist on reward, with rapid abandonment of Underwritten Production, in the face of declining returns on Investment. More has to be rewarded with Dividends confronted with constricted Consumer Demand. Product price increases become automatic, generating a set level of Inflation. Business must alter its Investment schedules, because delays of Construction and Emplacement cannot be endured, with too great a period before return on Investment. Heavy Plant capitalization is abandoned in favor of quick return capitalization opportunities. Everything must be up and running, making a Profit, within a Quarter; else a low Profits Quarter will be registered. Long-term Capitalization of extended Plant becomes a thing of the Past, with such activity often switched Overseas or purchased from a foreign source. The Gross Domestic Product drifts toward quick Turnover Goods and Services, with avoidance of extended Infrastructure construction at low Profitability, unless the Government can be enjoined to fund it.

Study of the above trend in statistical methodology provides high indication it is pressured by current tax policy. Tax credits for Investment have been the vogue since the 1950s among Economists. Theory expounds that this enhanced Investment has been responsible for the listed economic growth of the last forty years. The Author disagrees sharply with this assessment. Capital aggregation is normally funded by payment of In-Step payments of the Production cycle. Measures to increase Investment, beyond the normal range of payment, only spur Inflation, through increasing financial reserves, in relationship to normal Production capital. A significant by-product is reduction of Consumer Demand, in attempts to minimize tax payment, and consist of reduced Wage increases to Labor, granting higher Profits which can be retained, due to the Investment credits. The End-result, as can be statistically proven, places Product-price increases ahead of the Curve, in comparison with Wage increases.

The Analysis explains the Scenario of the Economy We now face. We currently produce a greater GDP than any Nation in history. We are doing this when our production facilities only work at about 70 percent capacities. Soft Consumer Demand and Business response to it means our Economy has been engaging in production investment at rates somewhat less than 40 percent of potential for a period of almost five years. A Layperson may not fully understand the implications of this Scenario.

Existing Production capital is operating at only somewhat less than 70 percent of capacity. This means there is a dearth of Consumer Demand of almost 30 percent, this being only a cursory observation. Production investment schedules of less than 40 percent of potential means Consumer Demand should be much higher, potentially twice what it is Today. The cause of the absence of Consumer Demand relies solely on the current tax policy now in place, which provides tax credits for Investment in a manner most hazardously to Consumer Demand. The whole process need be examined!

Economists could explain that almost all Consumer Demand is derived from Disposable Income, which is Income denuded of fixed financial commitments, deriving mainly from Expenses for life maintenance—Mortgage payments, Utilities bills, educational expenses, work expenses, and payment of previous Consumer credit charges. The Layperson would say these denuded fixed financial commitments make up most of their individual Income, and most of the Economy, and they would be quite correct. It might seem more Consumer Demand comes from the fixed financial commitments, than from Disposable Income, but actually; little Consumer Demand derives from these charges.

Consumer Demand remains the desire for additional products, along with the ability to pay for such Products. Fixed financial commitments call for no additional Housing, Transportation, Electricity levels, Communication levels, or new Consumer products. They simply insist on the same minimal level of provision as enjoyed previously. Price increases in fixed financial costs means a personal Household inflation, as it costs more to retain original position. Disposable Income, on the other hand, means the potential for additional increments of Consumption. It provides for increased levels of Consumer credit extension, alongside the potentiality of paying cash for Products. Disposable Income provides almost all avenue for Consumer Demand as defined by Economists—whether Business or Household.

The above discussion does not exclude fixed financial commitments from providing additional Consumer Demand, as Consumers increase their consumption of such things as Electricity, Gas, Communications, and minimal payment of Consumer credit. Statistics indicate almost 7 percent of all Consumer Demand yearly comes from this source. It is a relatively consistent increase actually, differing markedly only in times of Boom and Bust; where there is a loss of approximately 2 percent of yearly Consumer Demand during the later. It is still not the beating heart of Consumer Demand, which is to be found in Disposable Income.

Consumer Demand's relationship to Gross Domestic Product is identical to that of the engine of a Car. Disposable Income cannot be likened to the fuel for the engine, more akin to the Octane rating of the Gas. Fixed Financial Commitments provide the greatest bulk of the fuel for Gross Domestic Product, but loss of the octane of Disposable Income starts the engine running rough, with a great decrease of power. Profits start to dissipate with drops of Disposable Income, with drops in Consumer Purchasing eventually bringing reduction of Fixed Financial Commitments; this occasioned by reduction of Productivity Schedules due to constriction of Consumer Demand. Loss of growth in Gross Domestic Product will come with loss of Disposable Income, and reduction of Fixed Financial Commitments actually means real loss of Gross Domestic Product. Growth of GDP can be gained without an increase of Disposable Income, but it is an imaginary growth, totally dependent upon increased Costs of Production. A set or decreasing Disposable Income insures eventual decline in Fixed Financial

Commitments. This decline means a static GDP, due to loss of financial and Productive profitability.

The Economy requires an increasing Gross Domestic Product, under the scenario of an expanding labor force. The increase is necessary to provide Work opportunities to Labor, and supply additions of Population with basic life maintenance products and services. Failure of this provision is the true definition of Recession, though almost all Economists would disagree with this evaluation. They would claim the Used Product markets provide life maintenance for increases of Population, and increased Unemployment does not inflict recessionary conditions. Actual fact dictates such conditions cause actual aging of Capital and Product, with worsened standards of living and loss of aggregate wealth. Apparent well-being does not assure that the Patient is not dying! The terminal illness is only in the incubation phase. The Economy can only absorb so much static performance in the face of increasing needs, before all start to suffer.

The American Economy already faces an aging labor force, which presents another quite different economic hazard to be faced. Youth is necessary to perform many of the harder occupations of the Economy at peak performance. Business importation of labor to perform these harder tasks have two adverse implications. The first lies in the fact almost 2.1 labor dependents are imported along with each labor asset. This insists that Productivity must increase at a rate of 2.7 times the Productivity as each imported labor element. This maintains Consumer Demand, but depresses the long-range standard of living. The second demerit to importation of labor leads to the aversion of domestic labor to menial tasks, such leading to the long-term incapacity of the Economy to sustain itself. Importation of labor holds only imaginary advantage, and drafts long-term commitment of economic assets to supporting a larger indigent Population.

The Economy suffers from the current trend of increasing the individual benefits of a welfare system. Evaluation of the welfare system implies an increasing drift from individual contribution to the welfare system. The system also faces increasing expansion, due to increasing Population and award of benefits. This throws an ever-increasing burden on the Private Sector, to provide payment for such services. This reduces the Profits of Productivity, immaterial whether this payment comes through tax on Business Profits, Wages, Sales, or Property. Capital aggregation and total Productivity suffer decrease from maximization of Productivity. This means the Economy loses natural growth, in the face of increasing Government provision of welfare needs.

Most Economists waffle in discussion of the welfare system. A great number deride the extension of welfare services, but few advocate reduction of any current services, fearing Public reaction—the People demanding Bread and Circuses. None will discuss the most important area of control in this debate, which is an individual limitation of provided services. The American Public presents the image of a Lynch mob, whenever confronted by suggestions of curtailment of individual excesses. Current passage of the new Medicare reform introducing payment for Proscription drugs brings the specter organizational gouging of the system; the $400bn allocated gave $70bn to Doctors for assurance of being paid(when most are already overpaid), give Businesses some $30bn in tax credits for Proscription benefits to Retirees which they had already guaranteed to those Workers, and disallowed Medicare from negotiating with the Drug companies for Wholesale prices in bulk. The worst danger for Medicare is no Individual life-time limit on total Benefits, with organizational fraudulent practice coming in second

Certain questionable Economic studies based upon highly debatable data insist that Dollar effectiveness can be discerned between Private usage and Public usage of Funds. The upshot of the studies states that a publicly-spent Dollar has only about $.71 of the utility of a Private Sector expenditure of a Dollar. The Author does not know whether to agree or disagree, finding the evaluations questionable. He does note the diminished performance of Civil Servants, the slowed delivery schedules of Private Sector companies working under Government contract, and the sluggishness of Production Step payments by these companies. Another Economic study he puts more credence into defines a relationship between the weekly benefit per Welfare recipient and the weekly salary of the dispensing welfare agent; the greater the disparity, the greater length of time for resolution of all Paper issues. The Cost of such Paper issues rises as the period increases as well. This indicates Civil Servant labor decreases in actual value, with an increase in salary. The Author believes the original studies were right in the thesis, if not very evaluative conclusions of data.

Gross Domestic Product ratios obviously suffer from expenditures for welfare measures. The degree of this loss need not be assessed with complete accuracy, but simple acceptance of its existence is sufficient. Provision of welfare measures degrades the value of Labor, and therefore, the Wages paid for it; making Labor more unattractive, with menial tasks held in contempt. The type of welfare measure undertaken is also vitally important. Measures which leave open-ended benefit levels per Individuals are the worst—most notable being Medicare, Medicaid, and Housing subsidies. The reason for the foregoing lies in the automatic avenue for Inflationary pricing. The Case in Point made by the Author comes in the Salaries of Doctors, he knowing they are going to sentence him to die of some deadly affliction. Their efficiency has only increased about one-third since the date of the Author's birth, but their remuneration has increased by almost 680%; this countered by the fact their education has increased 500% in cost, and the fact everyone else has had a remuneration increase of almost 500% (except for the Author—then, now, or in-between). The relevant issue here, though, resides in the fact Medicare and Medicaid payments provided some estimated 200% of the increase in remuneration for both Doctors and everyone else. Such open-ended welfare benefits for Individuals produce Wage increases in Suppliers of Immediate Needs, and over the long-term throughout the Labor force, to counteract the free supply of services to non-laborers.

It is the Author's contention the effect does not increase the Gross Domestic Product, but actually contracts it, caused by inflationary pressures in the In-Step payment structure of Productivity. Almost universal Economic thought expresses the contention that Government expenditures actually increase GDP, through the provision of Goods and Services to the Public sector. The Author does not believe this, thinking the Private Sector to be far more efficient in provision of Goods and Services, within a spectrum where Labor Wages and Salaries are maximized, presenting the highest Consumer Demand possible. He actually believes Public Sector provision actually costs $1.37 of Private Sector Production, for every dollar of Pubic sector Product and Service more than 14.3 percent of Gross Domestic Product.

Chapter:
Inflation and Deflation

The above subjects occupy a paramount position in Economic discussion, and rightfully should, but little of the discussion revolves around the real impact of Inflation or Deflation. Inflation to the Layperson means Prices are going up, Deflation means Prices are going down. The Businessman sees Inflation as the ability to pass operational utility costs onto the Consumer, perceiving Deflation as inability to pass these operational utility costs unto the Consumer. A description of operational utility costs means seniority raises for Employees, incentive raises for Employees, medical and life insurance premiums for Employees, and retirement pension payments if they internally finance their pension plans. These required, or pressured, payments do not reduce; such payments become reduction of Profits in the absence of Inflation. Business Management finds such loss of Profits onerous. Economists witness Inflation and Deflation as increase or reduction of the Money Supply, or alternately; increased or reduced speed of Turnover of funds in the Money Supply. The Layperson may have the most common sense attitude toward Inflation and Deflation, due to the fact all others have talked themselves into viewpoints not readily explanatory, or capable of producing practical statistics or solutions.

Inflation does mean uniform Product Price increases, and Deflation does mean uniform Product Price decreases. This only begins the discussion of the subject, it does not end it. Inflation and Deflation must be viewed as equilibriums, and overall balance points at any given period of time. The Layman should think of a Scales, with one side of the Scales holding the total of Goods and Services, and the other side holding the Money Supply. Production of Goods and Services increases the weight of one side of the Scale, and Purchases of those Goods and Services lighten that side of the Scales. Each Good or Service, though, has a monetary value composed of the raw material cost, Capital cost, Labor Cost, and Profit from Production of the Good or Service. The monetary value is added to the other side of the Scales with every addition of Good or Service, and removed from the Scales with the removal of the Good or Service upon Purchase.

This exceedingly simplistic outline holds no real value, only to explain Inflation, or Deflation, are uniform Product Price levels balanced with momentary Money Supply levels; the importance resident in the fact they are balance readings, which are affected by increments of Goods and Services being added. They are uniform, or averaged Product Price levels, but this averaging alters by the additions of Goods and Services. The prices of Goods and Services vary on an individual basis, affected by the widely divergent forces. This highlights a very important Economic point: Inflation or Deflation is the residual reflection on the Macro level of the Economy, of alteration of Costs and Prices at the Micro level of the Economy. The Student will find these alterations are caused by the Intermediate Step Payments of the Production process.

The Author makes the previous statement because raw material costs, Wage costs, and Intermediate Step Profits all belong to these payments. Inflation and Deflation only occur at the end of the Production cycle, when the Producer decides to maintain, increase, or reduce his Profit margin on the Product, in reflection to alteration of Intermediate Step Payments in Production. The End-Producer is simply averaging his Costs, and assigning a Profit margin in setting Product Price. Examination of the Production Cycle, therefore, establishes the origins of Inflation or Deflation derive from the Intermediate Step Payments of the Production process.

Economists continually attempt to identify the exact causes for Inflation and Deflation. The best explanations always fall short of total clarity, as the Author expects this discussion will. The rationale for the failure lies in the complexity of motivations possible behind the Process of Price Increase and Decrease. The Author will attempt explanation of Inflation, then Deflation, followed by an attempt to unify the Two in an understandable pattern.

The Free Market system equates a limited supply of Product with the out-standing number of Consumers, distributing the Product based upon the monetary payment any one of the Consumers is willing to pay. The first of the Consumers willing to come up with the highest monetary payment gets as much of the Product as he desires. This can be altered by setting of Product prices by previous Contract or Government control of prices, basically either Inflationary or Deflationary in aspect—as it alters the nature of the Market. It can also be altered by the establishment of Monopoly conditions, Oligarchy being a Monopoly, entered into by the major Suppliers of a line of Product; both utilize their position to control Supply; thereby setting prices which produce economic profits(entrepreneurial profits plus added financial gain). The Free Market may or may not incite Inflation or Deflation, determined by the structural content of the

Market. Supply of Product can vary, due to various conditions of the Environment, Capitally utilized, Labor employed, and the rate of recovery and delivery. The number of Consumers can vary due to Population totals, and the amount of available Funds they possess with which to purchase the desired Products.

Product Price increases, bringing overall Inflation, have innumerable roots at the Product supply level. All impact upon the Free Markets process. Weather conditions may slow the rate of recovery or delivery of the Product. Capitalization costs of recovery or delivery may have increased; likewise, so can Labor costs. Diminishment of Ore may bring Ore price increases, or Capital Equipment cost increases may do the same for harder recovery measures for the Ore; or even more, delay the rate of recovery. Higher Costs for debt service for Capital can raise the price. Insistence on maintaining Profits margins under conditions of increased Costs can also raise the Product price. These are the Supply-side pressures generated to push up Free Market prices for the Products.

Demand-side pressures can also affect the Free Market pricing of Product. Increase of Consumers greatly effect the pricing of Product; remember that Consumers must not just be numbers, but Individuals with the ability to purchase through access to funding. Alteration of the methods of financing can increase Product prices, as traditional Consumers are willing to accept greater debt, or having received greater remuneration for their own economic production. Outside Participants may have entered the Market with dispersal of acceptable funds. Government may enter, and demand first priority for Product, thereby reducing levels of Product available. Resupply of previous Product due to losses also increases Demand, these losses due to Accident, Weather, or War.

Both Supply and Demand can vary readily, and Free Market pricing increases and decreases according to changes in the equilibrium. This remains a free-floating process with only one outlet to forestall Inflation or Deflation, this being Business willingness to alter their Profit margins to maintain Prices; this ability limited, in itself, by the needs of Debt service, Recapitalization, and Profitability. Monetarists suggest another alternative in regulating the cost of Debt finance, but they suffer from the effect of their own efforts; this Cost varies for both Supplier and Consumer, so the basic pressures remain unaffected. Such action can only delay Inflationary or Deflationary pressures, this at an increased cost to Debtors, or loss of Profitability to Lenders. Government setting Price schedules always fails, as it allows Inflationary or Deflationary pressures to build without release; ending in reduced levels of Productivity, or rapid Inflation or Deflation after removal.

Inflation allows Business to shove operational utility costs and Debt service costs off on the Consumer, through accelerated Product prices. One of the greatest factors in the increase of Management salaries and benefits comes in inflationary funding of operational utility costs, under the provision of paying themselves first. This can be identified by equating Percentage increase of Product prices to Percentage increases in Operation Costs. Management remunerations stand as the great absorber of inflationary price increases, with quickly expanding Salaries and Stock Options; while Dividends have been increasing at much more sedate rates. This is especially relevant as operational utility costs to Production of labor has been decreasing in percentage over the last Thirty years. It is indicative that expressed inability to shove Debt service costs off on the Consumer, quickly led to Business pressure on Government for tax exemptions and rebates to pay for such Debt service.

Inflationary effect on the Consumers has almost the opposite effect, as for Business. Static Incomes lose purchasing power. Wage-Earners get accelerated Wage packaging, but not equal to the Product Price advances, this causing a much slower loss of purchasing power. Those living on Interest and Dividends imagine some possible gain, but this gain does not equal the continuous Product price increases. The worst arena for all Consumers lies in the provision of Professional Personal Services, as Professionals insist on remuneration equivalent to the Product Price increases. Inflation, over the long-term, brings loss of standard of living to all but Business Management and Professionals; these maintaining their position only if they maintain an independent Service provision function.

Inflation has been called the hidden virus of the Economy, but Deflation remains the invisible Dark Horse, with few being able to identify root cause. Current speculation states the American economy may be entering a Deflationary period. The Author actually believes this is the case. Corporate Price schedules are set to maximize internal Corporate finance of Production and Operating Costs; this being marked Monopoly pricing. This is the cause of the current Deflationary pressure, though, which is basically oversupply for the Consumption dollar; this defined as the actual budgetary amount acceptable for Product purchase. This oversupply derives not from lack of Consumers, but from their inability to pay at the Product prices demanded. Production has been geared over the last two decades for the Affluent, while this segment of the Population—both in the United States and the World—have been over-served with Product. Production lacks Consumer Demand because of lack of Consumer finance, but Consumer finance which cannot be buttressed by traditional Monetarist measures. Consumption must be expanded in the less Affluent, and Consumer debt cannot apply; as the less Affluent do not possess capacity of further repayment on Consumer debt. The only Short-term possibilities for economic redress are reduced Production, or deflationary reduction of Product pricing, the long-term solution being gearing Production for the low-Income market.

Reduced Production is basically Recessionary, as it actually reduces the size of the Affluent, who can purchase Product at the Prices now charged. It does not increase the capacity of lower-Incomes to purchase Product at current pricing. Reduced Production will lead to under-funding of Recapitalization, extended Consumer debt finance with Demand-draining Interest charges, and increased demand for Government welfare services. Drastic Product price reductions need be introduced to speed the Consumption of the sated Affluent, and bring viable lower-Incomes into the Consumer Demand arena. The Author uses the term 'Drastic' because it is exactly what is meant; gradual Product Price reduction will renew Products for the sated Affluent, leading to Short-term gains, but long-term suppression of Affluent Demand. Viable lower-Income levels will be tied up in long-term Consumer Credit agreements, with suppression of long-term Consumer Demand from this segment. Growth of other lower-Incomes in Product Demand elements will therefore be slow, unless the Price cuts are drastic. The Author would offer as example the spectacle of $300 computers, and SUVs starting at $15,000; they currently start at $900 and $23,000 respectively.

The above discussion outlines a fact about Deflation, occurring in every circumstance where it is not too gradual over Time. Deflation will bring increases in the standard of living of the Population, due to the fact Wages decline much slower than Profits, and with an approximate ten-month delay behind Prices. Wages do not decline slower than Profits always, only when actual Production Profits are above 12 percent. The Author uses actual Production Profits as the term, to eliminate Management salaries and benefits, with no Accounting of the costs of Worker benefits like pensions and medical insurance. Wages actually decline 1.74% faster than Profits, at less than 12 percent actual Production Profits, this again a hypothetical Study. Employee Consumer Demand rates will actually increase without a threat of loss of Income, even in the face of declining rates of Wage, if substantial Bargain Product pricing is perceived. It must be remembered by the Reader that the above information is based only upon Economic modeling, as no actual Deflationary period of magnitude has been witnessed in the modern Economic setting.

The special case of slow, gradual Deflation should be examined to understand the corrosive nature to economic performance. Business, under these circumstances, manages to maintain their Profit margins, but at a sharp cost in economic performance. Labor benefits are sharply reduced, Downsizing increases, short-term Layoffs become more frequent with Vacation times eliminated, and Wages frozen in place. Consumer Demand contracts, both from loss of services to Labor, and from Labor forced to replace lost services—reducing their Disposable Income. Consumer Demand, therefore, decreases at a rate in advance of the rate of Deflation. The Reader should remember the worst effect of frozen Wages comes in removal of incentive raises; the impact of this is serious, causing an approximate .08% loss of Labor Productivity per Quarter, after removal of the incentives. This has a tendency to reduce Deflationary pressure under sharp deflationary conditions, but increases the rapidity of Downsizing and Layoffs under gradual Deflation, accounted by less Profitability of Plant operation per hour. Most may not be able to understand the undesirability of gradual Deflation, but all can understand reluctance of Business to promote a Product Price Sale of 5 percent; yet it is simply a reflection of the unviable economic nature of gradual Deflation. It does not goad Consumer Demand, while having very abusive effects on Productivity.

Much economic speculation and some Economic modeling have been done about Deflationary conditions. A tentative hypothesis indicates presence of any Deflation should lead Business to spur Deflation past 8%, to accelerate Consumer Demand by cheaper Product. This increased Consumer Demand is incited by lowered Profit margins, but the increase of Sale volume is expected to discount the loss of Profits, all within a forum of increased Wage payments to Labor. Rates of Deflation less than 8% per year will bring erosion of Profit margins in any case, coupled with losses of Productivity, paid Wages, and reduced Disposable Income for Labor. The Reader must remember this is highly speculative, with no Economist besides the Author, being willing to be so strong in pronouncements.

There may be some confusion as to direction of economic action which should be taken under the effects of Inflation and Deflation. Simplicity can devise a statement for Students to retain: Inflation should be starved, while Deflation should be fed! This means the rate of Inflation should be held as low as possible, while the rate of Deflation should be increased to where the fall of Prices brings increased Consumer Demand. The Economy can maintain maximized Productivity levels under conditions of heavy Deflation, and under conditions of gradual Inflation. It will immediately be obvious to the Alert that periods of Deflation will always be much shorter than periods of Inflation, except in the cases of gradual Deflation and Hyperinflation.

Gradual Deflation can extend to lengthy periods. This results in extreme loss of Productivity levels. The loss comes about through sharp reduction of Consumer Demand, basically because of huge percentage loss of Disposable Income. Debt service becomes more expensive, as it must be replaced at value-cost higher than when contracted. The Consumer faces little loss in Product Price, especially in area of Recurrent Costs like Utilities, with a heavier repayment burden for Capital debt. Labor Productivity is likewise dropping, along with less total Product produced and sold; so Business is losing Profits from both Labor and Capital, while their Static Costs are reducing at a much slower rate than their Profits. The Author's own sketch pad (no contempt expressed please!) suggests a One percent Deflation rate can cause a Nine percent loss of GDP over a Three-year period. A Deflation rate in excess of 8 percent, on the other hand, can be expected to incite at greatest a One percent drop in GDP over the same Three-year period.

The previous information, if true, is important in its own right, but its importance increases when considering the total impact of heavy Deflation. Consumer Demand will have been maintained, or increase due the heavy rate of Deflation. Recapitalization and Capital Investment rates will have been maintained, due to the consistent Consumer Demand. The previous two rates incite their own Consumer Demand and consumption of Resources. Some Economists, at least this Author, speculate the total Deflation cannot exceed 11 percent under conditions of continued Capitalization, without stabilization of the Money Supply; this means elimination of Deflation, and a probable return to gradual Inflation. The Reader must remember that the Author has little support for his conclusions among Economists, though some Few among them admit such circumstances could well be possible.

Hyperinflation, on the other hand, has had the attention of Economic investigators to a far greater degree. This special horror destroys Productivity because Capital and Production resources cannot be paid from Profitability of previous sale of Product. It actually becomes more profitable to withhold Product from sale, until future resource and Capital has already been purchased. The Student can understand how such delay could lengthen the Production process, and reduce Labor productivity profits to nil. The only profitable enterprise becomes the printing of money, if they have purchased their ink prior to forwarding of the Product. Economists love to discourse on the German citizen of 1923 taking a wheel barrow of Cash to buy a loaf of Bread; there is a little of the Demon in us all. Some Countries have seen Hyperinflation since that time, but it is rare, especially with the advent of the modern banking system; where most of the Money Supply exists in the form of Demand Deposits, which cannot expand at the same rates consistent with printing Currency. Hyperinflation will not be declared dead by the Author, though he will state that in the absence of extreme Government deficit spending; it is no longer possible(George W. Bush should be sent a Copy of this Work).

Inflation and Deflation are with us almost continually, due to the nature of Free Market forces. Most Economists would state the American Economy has been in a continuous state of gradual Inflation since 1933. The Author believes this statement highly suspect. It is his belief all Recessions are accompanied by gradual Deflation, but often hidden by Government deficit spending or Private Sector action, one artificially expanding the Money Supply based on no initial economic activity, the latter exerting heavy deflationary pressure through Bargain Sales for Product. The frequency of the latter Bargains exhibiting a need for decreases in product pricing, more frequent Sales for retail Product highlighting overpricing of Product causes insufficiency of Consumer Demand.

In-depth analysis should be made as to the root causes of Inflation and Deflation, but the Author uses only theoretical speculation, due to lack of funding for proper investigative tools. Milton Friedman and the Monetarists have shown some level of Inflation is incited by extension of Consumer Credit. The Author has previously shown most Inflation is caused by deficit spending by Government, increasing Consumer Demand without payment for that competition. Business also incites Inflation by Corporate Price schedules designed to produce economic profits, in excess of normal entrepreneurial profits. The Author has previously shown that long-term Inflation cannot be occasioned by Resource shortage or Technological Capitalization Costs, this due to the Averaging process of the Free Market through Generations of Product purchase to the entire Economy. This concludes Inflation is not caused by Free Market forces in operation, but only through abnormal economic practice; some of these abnormal economic practices, like the extension of Consumer Credit, actually increase economic performance and the standard of living of Consumers. Most other abnormal economic factors inciting Inflation actually retard economic performance, and should be removed. Their removal would vastly reduce the rate of Inflation.

The Author has many thoughts as to what incites deflationary pressures, untested due to lack of resource. His most persistent hypothesis, to which he gives greatest credence, states Products and Services are designed for a specific Target market, with Production geared to fulfill the Consumer Demand of this Target market. He must bring up the definition of Consumption saturation, where target Consumers hold sufficient Product of sufficient durability, that purchase of new Product at current Price levels is wasteful to Consumers' budgeting. Repurchase of Product by these Consumers will await aging of the Product at the current Price schedule. Business extension into a wider market will cost a loss of

Profit margins on the Product due to the cost of Advertising, while sales to the saturated Target market required Product price reductions of magnitude. The Consumption saturation is the deflationary pressure which brings on Deflation. Overall Economic Deflation rates occur when significant Target markets reach Consumption saturation at current Price schedules.

Other Factors could obviously also bring some Deflationary pressure, but only one could bring the level of pressure necessary to incite overall Deflation in the Economy. This consists of Government surpluses operating within the presence of heavy Government spending through heavy taxation. This equates to Government finally paying for previous Consumption, and thereby actually funding the Costs of Production of previous years; the entirety of the Process actually reducing the value-cost of Goods and Services to current Consumers, even though they must pay higher taxes. A great list of Economists would disagree with this assessment, but the reduction of value-cost of Product comes through lower Interest rates on Consumer Credit, lower cost of Production Capital, lower costs of Production materials, and lower Business Profits margins due to Competition where Operational Costs are lower. An Overview dictates there is Deflation because of less pressure on Resources and Productive capital; otherwise stated, fewer Consumers of Product leads to lower Production schedules for Resources and Capital under terms of full capitalization.

Another component to Deflation could be the transference of Production Operations to a market separate from the Consumption market. This is only a temporary short-term condition, though, because of the Averaging Process of the Free Market. The cost of Production in foreign markets will increase, and Transport Costs to move the Product will increase, while Consumer Demand will decrease in the home market. This is a much more rapid process than most would perceive, with Averaging accomplished within the Fifth Generation of Product Sales. This remains less than a Four-year period for most Products. Such Export of Production actually should become Inflationary for the home market within Seven years, and within the Importing market within Three years. The threat of Export of Production Operations is not a long-term threat to home markets, especially not One of magnitude like the American Economy.

The effects of Inflation and Deflation have been examined, probably to the disgust of more traditional Economists. They are structural stresses inside the Economy, basically established by abnormal operation of the Free Market, remembering artificial stress can promote economic performance in some instances. Neither Inflation nor Deflations are innately evil, as the Author once titled a book about Inflation, but both can adversely affect economic performance if left untreated at adverse levels of development. The Reader must remember Economic performance remains a balance of forces, balanced in the Free Market Averaging Process. This Averaging can be distorted by non-Economic considerations based on Government action, or utilization of monopoly positioning and pricing in the Economy by Private agents. Do not be condemnatory, as the Union and Professional can be as guilty, as can the Businessperson or Politician. Economics is not a Study of assigning Guilt, but one of maintaining economic balance for economic performance.

Chapter:
Distribution of Income

Anathema for any Conservative comes with the discussion of Distribution of Income. The basic Conservative position states Income is distributed by the Market system, in pursuit of Productive skills and Capital. It seems like a straightforward proposition, but it most certainly is not; this Chapter devoted to discovery of its error, as well as the effects of mal-distribution upon Consumer Demand. The basic thesis of this Work can be contained by the statement: Almost 60 percent of current distributions of Income by the Market pay for past Productive effort, not current or future efforts. This does not imply distributions are made for last Week's work, but involvement in the Economy in years past, factors which allowed for an equivalence to monopoly positioning in current Management for Production. This monopolization of Productive controls lead to dysfunctions within the process of Production, and adversely trims the produced Consumer Demand. The result brings loss of standard of living and economic protection for almost all Participants within the Economy.

The Author would first desire to state he is not an opponent to Interest, or Capital Gains, the main motivations behind the aggregation of Capital. It is a point in fact that he would enjoy more secure placement of both within the Production Process. Such security possesses ease of implementation, simply requiring a change in Accounting procedures used by Business. Both should have a place in Production Costs scheduling, not simply in Profits Distribution scheduling. Each should be monitored as Production inputs, as are Labor and materials. The Lay Reader may not understand this Concept. Just like Labor is awarded an hourly Wage, so too should Interest on Capitalization or Capital Gains be awarded an hourly or per Piece wage. Requiring this change in Accounting would be simple, direction by Congress or IRS would be sufficient.

The effects of this Accounting alteration would be profound. Business first could not hide unprofitable Production lines, within an internal Profit-spread across all Production lines. Business would be compelled to make Production scheduling decisions based upon the actual potential profitability of the Product, not Blue-Sky projections based on Management desires other than the Profit motive. Production Costs would have to be stated clearly for both Tax Agent and Stockholder. Business will say Interest, but not Capital Gains, could be accounted in this manner. This would be a patent lie. The Law or regulation could simply be mandated to express an 8% return of Capital Gains on Production, whether it is computed by hours of Production, or on a per-Item basis. Production scheduling decisions will be required to be estimated, based upon these calculations, which will have to be presented to both Stockholder and IRS. The Author estimates 43% of all unprofitable Production operations will be closed substantially faster under such Accounting, and some 23% of Production operations will not be started because of shown unprofitability.

There will entail much less disturbance within the Economy, if the above estimates prove true. Numbers of Layoffs will probably be cut in half, and Downsizing may become a dinosaur, as Workers will not be hired in the first place. Job security by Workers alone should raise Consumer Demand by an estimated 9 percent. Most Economists would discount this Claim, but ignore the increased extension of Consumer Credit by financial institutions, at lower rates of Interest because of reduced Risk. They also neglect the greater percentage ratio for Household capital aggregation by lowered disparity between Income parameters for Households. Job retention will lengthen, and so; demands for medical insurance and pension benefits will increase. This pressure will increase Disposable Income levels of Households, while reducing immediate Wage levels; this under the Scenario that Business can provide such Services at less total Cost than can Individuals or Households; as component of Production Costs—Labor. Consumer Demand will obviously increase at significant rates.

Business losses should reduce with the proof of the above estimates. Risk will be removed from Capital Investments, as Investors will possess a much clearer understanding of Management projections. They will perceive less need for excessive Management salaries and benefits in order to protect their investment; so Management pay will begin to fall in line with other Production payments. Investors will be unlikely to see said funds return to their Profits. A simple diversion to Employee medical insurance and pension benefits will occur; yet, this will increase Consumer Demand. Investors will be rewarded by understanding that creditable Marketing research, will raise the safety factor of their Investments to an equitable par with financial instruments such as Bonds and Certificates of Deposit. This safety means actual increased skill in Production decision-making, bringing overall improvement in Production practice and Management.

The applicability of the above information to this Chapter is slight, except for the remission of disparity in Income levels in society. This disparity between Income levels in Society should reduce by 30 percent, with greater concentration around the Mean; meaning Highs and Lows will disappear, closing the distance between Income Average and Income Mean. Any Economist will tell the Reader that this closing of distance can be considered complete gain in Consumer Demand. The average Standard of Living increases as Income Average closes on Income Mean. Will there always be disparities between Income levels? Absolutely! Different levels of participation in Production utilizing different Skill levels, insures there will always be disparities. It is in the interest of the Economy, though, because of the effects of this disparity in Income on Consumer Demand, to limit this disparity to actual differences of Skill and participation, not allowing artificial disparities based up control or influence over Production decisions.

Conservative reaction to Income Distribution transfers by Government has been heavily documented by Spokespersons for their Interests. It remains amusing to Economists, who know how heavily the American Economy depends on such Transfers. The largest form of such Transfers stands as Social Security benefits, which turn into Income distribution transfers as soon as the Beneficiary exhausts what he has paid into the program. This requires an incredibly short interval of Payments—this Author suggests an average of 3.7 years(not counting an interval accrued Interest since Withdrawals) without consideration of Medicare payments (though this Period has been lengthening since the revisions of Tax payments upward), this stated without resort to official Government documentation. The average period of Benefits under Social Security must be in excess of Twelve years, though the Author cannot be sure. Medicare Recipients receive a level of paid care equivalent to a medical insurance policy with $4000 a year premium, for a total payout of approximately $400 per year, and about the same Deductibles as would be present with the private medical insurance. Some Government Economists have hinted to the Author that Medicare coverage would end in an average eleven months, if dependent upon what the Beneficiary had paid in as Medicare premium. The Author is not opposed to the Social Security program. He is simply stating Conservatives should not be so adamant in rejection of such transfer payments, because of their total refusal to include the Social Security programs as such Transfers. He additionally stipulates there is great incentive to introduce a standard Monthly benefit, not determined by payment levels into the system, as all Recipients generally exceed the total largesse of those tax payments into the system.

A uniform monthly Social Security benefit of only one size would reduce Administration costs of the system by 45%. It would increase Consumption levels of more than 40 percent of the Beneficiaries by some amount in excess of 20 percent of current Expenditures. The reduction of potential Consumer Demand by current high benefit levels would be negated by substitution of private Income held by the Beneficiaries, with Consumer Demand loss less than 10 percent (Author's estimates). Total Consumer Demand gain, in terms of purchase of Goods and Services, would equal an increase of almost One percent of GDP. Real term construction in Economic terminology would state such a uniform benefit would be an actual reduction of Income Distribution transfers by Government, though it is thought the Conservatives would not be pleased. Honesty must admit this would only lengthen the period before Beneficiary tax payments would cease to fund Benefits. The actual Dollar cost of such Payments would increase over Time, though tax payments into the system by Workers could lengthen the period under which the Social Security Fund was solvent. (The Reader may not realize current Workers would be paying higher taxes for less future benefit).

The Author must present the most important point for salvation of the Social Security Fund, along with the bloodletting of Government tax revenues. Medicare and Medicaid insurance must be outsourced to private medical insurance. This outsourcing would immediately bring about limitation of medical coverage, so Readers should beware of the Wolf in Sheep's clothing. The Government would outline the basic Coverage desired for the Policies, and put these Policies up to bid by private medical Insurers. The Government would determine the basic Coverage demanded, by the cost of competitive bidding, Congress setting the total yearly amount acceptable for such Coverage.

The benefit of such outsourcing is immense. Some 85 percent of the administrative cost of the Medicare and Medicaid programs would be shifted to the private Medical Insurers, who already have in-place staffs. Doctors would realize what medical services could be provided, and would discontinue discussion with Patients and their families of Procedures not covered under the policies. Levels of treatment would be designed within the limits of insured Coverage. Medicare and Medicaid coverage would become a Dollar distribution as premiums to private medical Insurers, along with a checkup to assure that Coverage was actually being given. A most important point resident in this proposition comes in the form Congress will be the determinant of the viability of the Social Security Fund. 'The Reader must recognize this is reduction of medical coverage to levels of acceptable cost, and extensive medical procedures will be reduced; though medical care will actually improve in terms of what is Cost-effective. This means, though, that Granny will likely die some Ten years sooner.

The above discussions in this Chapter outline several effective measures to redistribute Income in this Country, without any resort to Government transfers of any kind. Forced Accounting of Interest and Capital Gains as elements of Production Costs, will shift Labor costs from Management salaries to Labor wages and salaries, at an approximate rate of 6–8% per year; until Management salaries and benefits have lost 50 percent or more of their current value. Interest and Capital Gains payments will be more highly secured, and Profits will probably gain some estimated increase of Two percent per year during the Process, with a likely .75% increase thereafter, based upon the greater efficiency of Productive decision-making. The uniform Social Security benefit removes inflationary pressure from the system (cutting such generated pressures by an estimated 70%), while increased Consumer Demand will likely curtail any tax rate increases for the program. An outsourcing of Medicare and Medicaid coverage cuts Government administration costs, and eventual funding costs of the program. It will additionally impel a reduction of overall Medical Costs in the Economy, with a switch to Private Consumption, raising Consumer Demand, and actually increasing Employment in the medical industry while reducing the excessive Wage levels in the sector. The above suggestions alone could eliminate Thirty percent of the disparity of Incomes between Rich and Poor in this Country.

Another factor of potential value in eliminating the disparity between Income levels in this Country resides in the Government revision of their Contracting procedures. Institution of across-the-board Contracts for Government supply remission to Cost+8% schedules would eventually lead to a 30 percent Wage reduction in the Military/Industrial complex, with 80 percent of this remission coming from Management salaries and benefits. Other Suppliers of Government would endure about half the impact as the Military/Industrial complex—dependent on the level of technological Production entailed, but with the split between Labor and Management about the same. The Reader must recognize these are the estimates of the Author, and few other Economists are conducting any investigations in the specified areas at the present. Part of the rationale of this Work is to generate economic evaluation of the above estimates.

The Reader, at this point, may have derived an intuition concerning the Distribution of Income. Forced Transfers of Income, whether by Government or other Agent, do not work; only inciting inflationary pressures produced by those taxed, to maintain the full-value payment for their contribution to productive effort. The easiest manner this is accomplished comes in the form of Businesses serving the Income transfer Recipients, who raise their charges to the Recipients to increase their own profitability. This is quickly matched by Overall pricing, so the income transference does not affect the balance of economic effort. This Process can be economically mapped; the best scenario being Income transfers translate into 100% Inflation within 7.1 years, most cite a much longer time-frame, none less than 5.4 years; realism stating the flow of Inflation has some maxima, but not some minima of terminal length.

> [The Layperson need remember Inflation is the increase of Money Supply without an increase in Product. Both are increasing Supply values, ofttimes requiring complex equations after intense Mathematica computation. Inflation being accredited as increased largesse of Funds. It is quite accurate, just an alternative Economic view of Inflation.]

The real arena to alter Distribution of Income lies not in Government Income transfers, or even Unionism, it resides in the area of business regulation. Income redistributing calls for alteration of the manner in which Business and Production occur. Effective Government intervention for Income redistribution devolves into establishment of standard Accounting procedures and Tax policy. Government-instituted Accounting procedures imposed on Business can vastly reorient the payment schedules for Production as noted above. But it required more than the simplicity of Minimum Wage laws or mandated Employee medical insurance. Such laws regulate such activity to a Production Cost, with the payment for such transfers shifted upon others, mainly within a median of Inflation. Income redistribution demands a percentage of the Profits of Production, for real-value redistribution of Income to take place.

The Author has mentioned some of the more valid Accounting procedures which could be emulated without undue Business opposition. A more controversial method would be Graduated Capital Gains taxation, based on the relative size of posted Profits. Economic studies have indicated some 31% of all Business profits would shift to Labor wages and benefits under such a system, due to Labor demand for such, while Business refusal would only lead to taxation of Profits. Wealthy elements, though, would be forced to endure the same percentage rates of taxation as Labor, with resultant screaming of inability to aggregate resources for Investment. The Author must admit there is some truth in such an Accusation. The effective alternative is to set an economically viable set rate of taxation for Capital Gains—the Author suggests nothing less than 22%, and nothing more than 28%—with low set Investment tax credits; Author-suggested levels of $50,000 per Individual, and $250,000 per Business or organization as maximum tax credit levels. It would not only vastly increase Government tax revenues, but Economic studies indicate approximately 12% of Business profits would transfer to Labor wages and benefits. The same Studies suggest no loss of Capital Aggregation.

Another Government tax procedure would be in a limitation of tax deferment for Management salaries and benefits. The Reader could find the following hard to understand, except by example: A law could be passed with stated: no more than 12% of Business profits could be deducted at Production Costs, in payment of Management salaries or benefits. Management reimbursements could be higher, but subject to tax as Corporate Income, and including all forms of Management payment, including life insurance, pension benefits, Stock Options, as well as Salaries. It would mean a modest decrease in Management reimbursement, mainly in the form of lowered Introductory salaries and pension benefits, and lack of pay raises for Management—less than a 3% loss per year (Author estimates). The long-term benefit of such law would be to transfer another 7% of Business profits to Labor wages and benefits.

Another law, which the Author favors (absolutely no chance of passage), concerns the elimination of parasitic class activity; the Author sounds like a rabid Socialist, does he not? Maybe, maybe not! This is not a forced labor law. It simply says: Everyone who has an Income greater than would a Minimum Wage Laborer working 2000 hours per year to a factor of five times, must pay Income tax over and above set rates to the level of Income cited; unless the Taxpayer can prove 2000 hours of gainful labor in the year, in which his income was earned. The Author is not after the working Rich, only their children and other dependents. Most Readers would think this law stupid, but several economic benefits can be cited: projected additional revenues would replace 7% of the tax paid by Incomes of less than $85,000, if it included Retirees; it would produce additionally several million hours of Productive labor in order to avoid the tax; and would increase Consumption by a projected 8%, without apparent Inflation. The Tax would affect only those who could afford it, and eliminate Social Security benefits and costs paid to those who do not need those benefits. The final Coup would be the forestalling of loss of valuable Labor assets due to laziness; while all Retirees could afford to retire when necessary. [Before being asked about it, the Author would state full-time enrollment in Education would be deemed to meet the requirement.]

Other measures could be devised to change the Business profits' distribution in this Country, but Supply-Siders have already determined this is a Socialist tract. The manner in which Income redistribution could be affected has been outlined. Reaganomics implanted the creed, and Greed is Good' as philosophy in our land, but it is suffering erosion, as the ranks of the Poor increase. It's gains prolongation because much of the Poverty is hidden: the hospital stays average $20,000 per week period; Dental reconstructions average $5,000; Clothing needs (New) average $2000 apiece per year; Household supplies average better than $1000 per year; Appliance replacement average yearly cost is in excess of $1000, and Utilities average some $3000 per year. The astute Reader will notice the discussion did not include Cars and Transportation, Rents or Mortgage payments, Fuel requirements, or Food. Judgement can be utilized about the Costs of Entertainment, school tuition, Restaurant eating, and jogging shoes. Most Working Poor cannot even afford the current cost of Coffee breaks, if taken at speciality Coffee Shops. There is no doubt there will be a redistribution of Business profits for the purpose of Income Distribution. It is only the question of what Poverty level will be endured, before such Changes are mandated. This remains no call for Revolution, as Conservatives claim; as the Author is closer to the Haves than the Have-Nots, though his Income remains dismal. It is simply a grasp of reality!

Chapter:
Business Opportunity

This section will essentially anger Conservative thought as well as previous passages. It will be an examination of the current economic system, as it is set up, with analysis why Consumer Demand is bound to fail under current business operating conditions. It will anger these Business Interests to a greater degree, when it is explained this failure derives from the Business modus of operation, which eats its own tail. A precise statement should be made at this point: Consumer Demand fails because Business refuses to share the Profits of Production with Labor, Government, or even Stockholders. Read further for detailed discussion!

A modern economic system remains dependent on technologically-specialized Production facilities. These facilities entail a high level of Capitalization, which in turn; it necessitates a high level of Product produced at an operating profit per item able to repay Capitalization cost plus Debt service charges. The high levels of Production required a highly-trained Labor force, and a huge Marketing capacity. Capitalization cost engenders Marketing problems, as Price is raised to pay the stipulated Costs. The first Problem of the modern Production process has appeared, Marketing Costs easily come to equal or exceed Production Costs; said Capitalization of Marketing services becoming a paramount expense, further driving up Product price. The dis-economies of Business operations begin to appear.

Business finds itself with shrinking Profit ratios. They need a vast Market for their Product, at Prices which will pay off the Capitalization of both Production and Marketing. Business seeks to minimize Costs everywhere possible, while seeking to expand Market outlets; this to draw in more Consumer purchases. Business finds Capitalization Costs, set by Business enterprise, cannot be materially reduced. Business cannot reduce Marketing Costs without a programable loss of Market Share. Business cannot raise Product Prices without a loss of Sales. Materials for Production cannot be effectively reduced in Cost, due to exterior Business enterprise maintaining Materials pricing. Business study their operation, and determine the only real reductions of Costs come in the form of reduced wages for Productive labor, reduced Dividends for Stockholders, and reduced Debt service charges.

Reduced Debt service charges have almost no impact on Capital Aggregation, though most Economists would claim otherwise. Government operation maintains a Money Supply of a magnitude capable of supplying Business operations' needs, while Political lobbies by Business insure Debt service charges can be reduced to acceptable levels. Business finds limitation to this venue, though, as Debt service (Interest) never averaged more than about 8% of total Product cost, at Production levels acceptable to Business. The functional elimination of Debt service (Interest rates at one percent or less), still presents an average Two percent of the total Product cost, at acceptable Production levels. The Six percent differential is meager gain in the face of Business need to cut Production Costs.

Marketing Costs express little expectation of ability to build Business profits. The limited Income of Consumers limits their Purchases, even with the extension of easy Credit terms. They must have levels of Income capable of paying off those Credit terms. Increased Sales means expansion of Market arenas. Start-up Costs in expansion of Markets are heavy frontal Costs, with a three-year delay before full Consumer performance. Market expansion is highly expensive in the Short-run, and runs into limitations in the Long-run, with expansion of Marketing structure costs eating up Profits made from expanded Sales. Markets reach saturation, as Consumers are continually supplied with durable Product. Increased Production to attain Production Profits loses viability.

Business turns to the venue of Productive labor payment. Here they do not face unified Business enterprise, adamant Consumers, or loss of Sales with diminished Marketing Costs. Business starts to erode the benefits given to Employees, which is a relatively High-Cost item structure, as these are supplied by other Business enterprise. Business continues to restrict Wage and Salary rewards, both for Seniority and Incentive. It continues until Business reaches the process of 'Downsizing', which is nothing but the substitution of experienced Labor with inexperienced young labor elements; to avoid higher salaries and benefits demanded by experienced labor. The Standard of Living of Productive labor starts to erode, but the element most important; Disposable Income of Productive labor contracts at almost three times the rate as the loss of the Standard of Living.

Elemental to the process of Productive labor loss of Standard of Living and Disposable Income is the switch occurring in expenditure patterns of Consumers. Consumers may basically double the length of time between purchases of durable products. They often switch to pre owned Products rather than new purchase, because of contraction of average Disposable Income. It is the reason why decline in Standard of Living is so much slower than decline in Disposable Incomes. The Process has suddenly become a disaster to Business, though Business fails to realize the impact.

Business organization wants for a systematic redesign. Business capitalization should alter orientation, moving from maximization of Sales, to capitalization of Production capacity for a minimal constant share of the Market. This alteration will minimize total Capitalization Costs, maximize Market Cost advertising, consistency and speed Product sale outputs, increase Consumer Demand for the Product, and reduce Inventory costs. Product price should be estimated at Production Cost at level of Overtime pay. Sale of Production at minimum share of the Market estimate or less will produce the extraordinary Profit per item to pay for Capitalization Costs, while Product sold at levels greater than 'least market share', can be produced at Profit with enhanced Labor Consumer Demand. The Business has sound capitalization, and with improved Marketing venues.

Capitalization Cost savings remain hard to formulate, the Author estimating anywhere from 4% of total Capitalization in this Country, to an estimated 17% of Capitalization. The difficulty in estimation comes between First-Round and Second-Round Capitalization, and the differential between the new equipment of First-Round capitalization, and the used equipment purchased in Second-Round capitalization. It is a question of the value of used equipment purchased, when First-Round capitalizations fail. An absolute discount of First-Round capitalization would give a figure in excess of 17%, with equipment versatility subtracting from this amount.

Marketing Costs savings would be almost double the ratio of Product sold per total Advertising dollars. Consumer Demand would be maximized with a waiting list of Customers for Product, because of an initial shortage of provision. It would be maintained by a continuity to the Advertising, though this Advertising would be at less total outlay. Establishment of a Consumer preference for the Product would allow for re-targeting of Advertising, to develop new Consumer Demand in new areas, while Production Costs are still funded.

Recessionary conditions would have minimized impact on such an organizational structure. Normal conditions allow for higher payments to Labor, enhancing their Consumer Demand, maintaining the economic environment. Discretionary Income is the prime component of Consumer Demand increases; it is in this area of Income where new, rather than replacement, purchases are made. Discretionary Income enjoys a boundary position in total Income. This means added Income is all Discretionary Income, in the absence of Static Costs increases. Labor operating under Overtime conditions often quadruple Discretionary Income levels. Smart Business personnel adjust their Production schedule to accept some comfort level of Overtime for Employees, without automatic thought to hire new personnel to minimize Labor Costs.

The combinations of the above conditions deriving from the Business reorganization remain hard to estimate. The Author expects Production Costs could be reduced by 20 percent. He also estimates Business could get double the Product sold for equal total of Marketing. Capitalization Costs would be guaranteed payment with abusive Cost-cutting procedures. Labor Costs could be minimized by lower Wages and offered Benefits packages; Overtime labor would make the Benefits cost-effective, while Labor would be happy with their enhanced Discretionary Income. The Author estimates the total increase in Profitability could range between 35–200% above Operations mounted in the old manner of Product maximization.

SECTION III

Chapter

The Reader now has a fundamental outline of the forces affecting the Economy. He understands Production must be established through the Profits of Production, coming as a result of Consumption of Product, realizing Production produces both Production and Consumption. Actual Capitalization operates through the In-Step Payment process of Production, with delays of said In-Step payments increasing the cost of Production. End-Consumption of Product simply pays the entrepreneurial profits of Management and Stockholder, with Production Costs already funded by the In-Step payment process. Management, itself, has to make a Capital return, in order to pay a return to Operating Funds or Stockholder; else Production funding will not continue. Production, therefore, becomes dependent upon Consumption; it standing dependent on Consumer Demand—Consumers willing and able to purchase Product. Consumption remains the driving necessity of Production.

Market forces now enter into play. Product must have a relationship to the Costs of Production and the final Cost of the Product. The price of the Product must also have a relationship with Consumer Demand. The price of the Product cannot be so excessive as to reduce the Population of Consumer Demand, those willing and able to pay. Price cannot be so small it fails to pay for the Capital Costs of Production, with sufficiency as to grant effective Profits for sustaining Production. Effective Profits can be perceived as the minimal amount of Profits necessary to incite Management of Production to continue Producing. Market forces decide if Product has genuine desirability capable of sustaining Production.

Government and Business policy and practice vitally impact on Market forces. Government policy can restrict desirable Product, through regulatory constraints on actual Production, or through targeted taxation. Government practice can also do the same, through poor Tax policy or mis-impacted regulation of Production. Business can utilize a union of desired Consumption and restriction on Capital construction(composed of Capital Cost, control of Resources or Technology, and/or criminal behavior), to impose Monopoly pricing, the practice of limiting sale of Product, creating artificial high Pricing for the Product. Business can also achieve Monopoly pricing at the Market Supply curve, through using a percentage of the economic profits derived; to create Consumer Credit funding, this exciting Consumers with desire to purchase above their original willingness to pay, because the long-term Product Price and Cost of Credit are hidden(in economic sense, hidden means the impact of such charges are delayed and spread so the Consumer believes he is gaining advantage). This practice is very popular, as Consumers do not understand Product Price increases are driven by the need to finance Consumer Credit, not Production Costs.

This Chapter will work only on limitation of Government policy and practice, in order to insure maximization of Consumption. The following Tax Provision will be introduced.

> **Consumption taxation, including what is commonly known as Sales taxes, will not be allowed at the Federal level. Congress suggests lower Jurisdictions repeal all such taxes. Such forms of Taxation retard the flow of Consumption and Trade. Congress reserves the right to impose Excise taxes on specific Products, in order to raise revenue or limit consumption of such Products. Congress specifically requests inferior Jurisdictions to limit their taxation measures to Income taxation, Property taxation, and Excise taxation.**

This Provision alters the basic Tax systems currently in force, as the knowledge-able Reader can understand. This Chapter will explain exactly what it does, and why it should economically do so.

Consumption taxes are highly prized by most Economists, as they are hidden taxes; forms of tax, which do not have to be closely budgeted, requiring no 'lump-sum' payments; Consumers are never faced with the total cost of taxation. This Author finds such taxes horrid for exactly the reasons cited, and for the economic detriment incurred. Voter, Taxpayer, and Consumer all fail to perceive the constant drain upon their resources; they sold a bill of goods, as to the 'non painful' nature of such taxation. Their apathy may or may not be desirable to both Politician and Economist, but the economic consequences of such taxes are a concern to all.

Consumption taxes depress Boom cycles, and deepen Bust cycles. Governmental authority gains unwarranted levels of tax revenues in Boom conditions, and sharp contractions of tax revenues on the other end of the spectrum. Consumption taxes are highly regressive taxes, impacting all elements of Society; even those Beneficiaries Government has sought to underwrite by Welfare transfers. Wealthier Incomes find tax advantage, as their restricted numbers present far fewer tax revenues presented, though their expenditure pattern can be much higher than normal. This tax regression seriously hampers Households in the aggregation of Household capital, while providing added tax shelter for wealthier Households. Examination of the economic effects of Consumption taxes expresses more economic distress.

Every Household must pay for Consumption taxes, most through the operation of Sales taxes on Consumer Products. One of the most noteworthy aspects of Sales taxation lies in Business practice of always rounding up at the Cash register. This occasions a much heavier tax than the stated percentage. Most Readers laugh at this comment, thinking it is nothing; except this nothing may cost American Consumers about ($380?) million dollars per year. This amount is a totally insignificant, minute aspect of the Sales tax problem, upon which the Author will discourse. The Reader may come to understand the impact of Sales taxes.

Consumption taxes target the wrong element of Consumer Income. It specifically targets Discretionary Income of Consumers, and utilizes their Fixed Costs to tax them. The economic sense of the argument can be expressed in a manner which is not exactly accurate, but presented for ease of comprehension: An economic model can be constructed where Income is static, Fixed Costs are static, Recapitalization Costs are static, and Consumer Products are static(static meaning no relevant change). The introduction of a Sales tax will eventually decrease the Standard of Living for the Household over time, due to a tax on all Living Costs within the Household. The Household must seek further Income to maintain their lifestyle. The Household will face rising those Living Costs, because all other Households and Businesses themselves face rising Operational Costs. This is not a modest increase in Living Costs either; a two percent Sales tax will lead to a Living Costs inflation of 8 percent per year, past the fifth year of implementation.

Most Economists would deride the previous analysis, but Households have been enduring serious loss of Income parity since the implementation of Sales taxes in the 1960s. A single-Income Head of the Household in 1960 could support a Family of Four in an independent Household. This Household had the advantages of full medical, Property, and Life insurance, could pay all Utility and other Fixed Costs, and enjoyed more Disposable Income in terms of percentage of Income for Entertainment. The Head of Household from this Period also has fully funded Pension plans with full medical insurance. Sales taxes and Corporate Income tax evasion compose the two chief elements of the current Retrograde from the Period.

Consumption taxes impact Consumer Demand equally as much. A 6 percent Sales tax rate will degrade Tenth year Consumer Demand by a minimum 60% of the First year's Consumer Demand, and probably at least 30% of the Tenth year's Consumer Demand. A Sales tax is not a benign tax. Most of the United States has endured a Sales tax for more than thirty years, with a degradation of current year Consumer Demand of 140% of the introductory year's Consumer Demand level. Households have probably lost One and one-half years of Productive Income from their capital accumulation, from the Sales tax imposed. The last thirty years have been hard on Households.

There are several amending protocols to the last information, the censure of the tax is reduced with increasing Productivity, which hides the loss of Household Income from the Sales tax. Governments would have raised tax revenues by other measures, which would have taxed the Household as well. The loss of Disposable Income may well have been lost in total, but the method of taxation is inherently bad! Households likely could have retained the advantages of the 1960 Household, rather than face the current circumstance.

Restriction of State and Local taxation to Property tax and Income tax allows for the unification of the tax system, where such payments can be deducted from the total Income tax paid to the Federal government. Excise taxation counteracts poor consumption decisions among Consumers, and should not be exempted in Federal tax; this only lessens the impact of the Excise, in place to limit consumption of Product at undesirable levels. The unification of the tax system allows for Averaging of Tax impact, similar to the Averaging process of the Market. Tax rates will reduce to a low Economy-wide average of least possible Tax impact. Tax revenue collection becomes a process of a purchased Product for the best Price.

Chapter

Standard Economic rhetoric stipulates Income revenues serve best, when they are individually reduced through Tax credits for investment. The Author states this is not 'Always right' embryonic declarative formalization. He believes Investment purposes remain better served by reduced tax rates, not Tax Credits for investment. This is not a Constant either, as there is the economic arena of promotion of Household aggregation, where Household Standard of Living is vastly improved over time by such Tax credits. Here is the Tax Provision derived:

> **Congress herein decrees all Tax credits, exemptions, or deductions from the assessed tax are null and void except for the following:**
>
> 1. **A normal Recapitalization credit of Seven (7%) per year on all depreciation property utilized within a Business organization. Averaging Accounting procedures will be used in assessment, but cannot be shifted forward or backwards in Tax periods; declaration must be made in the Current Tax Assessment Period Year.**
>
> 2. **Any Household or Business can employ a Tax credit of no more than $20,000 per Assessment Period Year, if they can prove an equal Investment in the same year; this only if the Tax credit does not exceed Twenty (20%) percent of the assessed tax after all other deductions, in the Period Year of Taxation. Twenty (20%) percent of the assessed tax can be received in any Period Year, except the numeral amount cannot exceed $20,000 per Period Year, unless Congress should declare an alteration in the numeral amount maximum.**

This Provision will provide great debate, as it contradicts established Economic thought on proper Tax policy.

The Recapitalization element of the Tax Provision will vitally alter the Accounting practice of modern Business. Accountants universally utilize sliding scales of Depreciation; a major component of value is tax evasion. Business pushes Recapitalization deductions forward to pay higher taxes in years of low Income; so they can avoid payment of Dividends to Stockholders or pay Capital

Gains by sole proprietorships. They then use these accumulated deductions to reduce total taxation in high Income years. The idea seems to hold benefit, but it does not! It costs tax revenues in both the tax period it was deferred, and in the year it was deducted. Business only accomplishes a reduction of their Operating Costs during the interval, which does not even equal the Interest on Operating Cost debt contraction, which remains a Business expense deduction. Both Government and Business lose inside a process, which allows minimal advantage of retained funds, but where Accounting and Administrative costs functionally nullify the advantage.

Businesses slide Recapitalization deductions backwards, in order to avoid tax assessments in high Income years. They hope to defray Start-up and Construction costs by this practice, using tax deferments derived in construction years to reduce tax payments in years of high Income. This is a highly successful practice for Business, often able to pay off Capitalization debt in major proportion. It allows use of flat Income years twice, once to avoid taxes in the year of taxation; then use the same year for a second year of tax evasion. Economists and Accountants join with Business personnel to proclaim this practice as beneficial for economic growth. It is not true! It cheapens the cost of capitalization—placing greater pressure and higher Price on Capital provision; placing a higher value on the Recapitalization deduction; most Economists insist Business enterprise desire the lowest-priced Resources and Capital Equipment. This remains true for the materials for Production, but is untrue for the cost of Capital Equipment; Interest payment on Capital debt defers the majority of payment unto peak Income years, and is tax deductible as Expense. The rate of Capital accumulation is delayed from a registry by existence of the Debt. Recapitalization amounts are also maximized in high Income years.

The rental property Businesses are among some of the worst offenders in the American economy. They purchase Rental properties for high Price, raise the rent on the Property to pay off the Mortgage and pay all expenses of Maintenance and Recapitalization, enjoy every Tax credit and other tax deduction including Interest on the Mortgage, and sell the rental Property for higher price upon payment of the Mortgage, quickly reinvesting so as to be untaxed under current tax credits. Such Businesses provide nothing to the rental Properties, except addition of another Mortgage. Renters, mostly unorganized, are left with Rents totally disport ionate to the housing provided. The identical practice is used in construction of these rental Properties, but the Business incurs the added effort of getting Renters.

The elimination of tax credits, except those stipulated, limits this Mortgage skating, as it is called in the Trade. Capital Gains will be taxed at full rates, without any allowance for investment, except for a paltry $20,000 per year, on massive-cost Business investments. Turnover of Property will insist on a high Tax cost, and Capital Gains will have to be paid on new constructions on Profits made over construction costs. A similar situation occurs for Productive industry. They will also be prohibited from riding on unpaid taxes paying for their Operating Costs; so they can permanently evade tax charges by expansion.

The entirety of the Economic and Business community will quickly insist this will ruin business initiative. This remains patently false! Most of American industrial history did not enjoy such advantages for Business. Income and Corporate Income taxes were not paid, but there was heavy taxation in Excises, Tariffs, and Property taxes. The Period between 1940 and 1963 witnessed high Business taxes, with probably the highest rates of economic growth of consistent proportion. Business taxes are not an automatic trammeling of economic performance. The Author, though, understands the effects of sudden Withdrawal from the Drug of Tax credits. The next Chapter will amend some of the 'Bends'.

Chapter

American Business possesses fixation on methodology to reduce tax payments. They abandon physical Plant because they cannot gain remission of Property taxes. They move out of areas where they have to pay excessive Unemployment contributions. They out source Production overseas simply because they have to pay Minimum Wage, Unemployment contributions, Utility use taxes, meet Environmental standards, and pay Local and State Income and Property taxes. They insist on tax credits for doing business in the only Market they possess, which has the magnitude necessary for their solvency. They feel victimized, if their advantages are reduced. The following Tax Provision is for the poor Business person, whose Standard of Living the Author is trying to destroy:

> **Congress herein revokes all Tax credits for Investment as previously allowed. The sole replacement as Tax credit for Investment will consist of a total deduction of all taxes paid by Employees of the Business in the preceding Year of Taxation to the U.S. Government, or to some subsidiary Jurisdiction within the land and territory of the United States. This numeral amount of deduction shall not exceed fifty (50%) percent of the estimated tax assessment, prior to the potential deduction.**

The Author smiles at the beauty of this Tax Provision, and the economic consequences of it.

The first Sentence cancels a half-century of Lobbyist efforts. The inequities of self-interest, long vested in Federal tax law, would be immediately voided, this without chance at justification by Special Interests. Introduction of a new Tax Code calls for the Sunset of the previous Code of Tax. The single Sentence tells all that new preferential treatment in the Tax Code must be negotiated, and realistically not liable to be maintained, especially when such preferential treatment lies in conflict with elements of the new Tax Code. All Lobbying effort and political contributions previously utilized to protect tax evasion will be nullified by the new Tax Code. Special Interests quickly recognize preferential treatment will require a complete refunding of Lobbying Costs, in order to reinstate tax advantage.

The Federal Government holds power to regulate the general economy, as stipulated by the United States Constitution. Current Congresses have instituted various Tax measures granting Tax exemptions and credits to American Business organizations, for Production operations in foreign Countries. It does not matter this Tax regulation does not mention foreign nations, the construct of the legislation allows Tax exemptions for a foreign outsourcing of Production. Argument could state this exceeds the constitutional power of Congress. The Argument is immaterial, though, because this practice neither regulates the general economy, nor does it promote the general economy. The Tax regulations allow serious disruptions in the flow of payments within the American economy, and loss of Capitalization.

It was mentioned earlier that Capitalization was not particularly a factor of aggregation of financial assets, which is most equitably done with modern financial instruments; Savings is not an effective instrument for funding Production. The switch to modern financial instruments, though, has an immense impact upon Capitalization. The End-Sale of Product loses all impact in development of financial assets for further Capitalization; it devolves into sole repayment of previous Capitalizations. Reinvestment of these repayments after End-Sale of Product is important to aggregation of financial assets; actually it is the sole medium for this aggregation, but only in a more refined context.

In-Step payments in the Production process are, in themselves, payments for Business organization End-Sales, but only as separate, distinct sub-Contractors to supply components of the Production cycle to the original capitalized Enterprise. Previous outlines showed the financial Capitalization function was fulfilled prior to End-Sale of Product. Actual recapitalization of Production has already been funded prior to this End-Sale of Product, by the In-Step payment cycle within the Production flow system. Study of this Process will insist more than 70 percent of all Production capitalization comes from the In-Step payments of Production. Transference of Production's to a foreign outsourcing eliminates In-Step payment contributions from the capitalization function, with redirection of capitalization funding to foreign nations.

The result of the previous named practice becomes contraction of actual hard domestic construction, with a proliferation of Stock and financial instruments within the domestic economy. This Paper replaces actual capitalization, but in an extremely damaging manner; it is equivalent to the practice of Government printing excess Currency. Less and less actual Production are actually done with domestic Labor, and payment venues for the Labor increase at a rapid rate. The value of those Paper instruments devalues rapidly, as the outsourcing of Production becomes increasingly expensive to purchase. Most Economists would insist exactly the opposite effect is occurring, but Employment roles are declining; Prices continue to rise, while return on the financial instruments and Stocks continue to decline.

The Tax Provision closes tax regulation which allows tax evasion for a foreign outsourcing of Production. Tax exemption is transferred from Investment to tax deferments for the employment of labor. It contains a philosophical implication that Business need not pay the taxes, which Employees have paid. The only methodology for tax remission comes through the employment of labor. Foreign labor, which does not pay American taxes, become functionally valueless for tax exemption. Downsizing and Layoffs become as financially restricting upon Business, as it has always been on Labor incomes. Pay raises, especially Incentive bonuses, cost far disfavor among Management; simply put, they will find it far more profitable to negotiate with, and work with, American labor. The advantage of a foreign outsourcing of Production has lost its advantage over domestic Production.

The last Sentence of the Tax Provision succeeds in closing another form of tax evasion; the tax farming of tax credits, deductions, and exemptions, so that no tax is paid. Business and Individual will not longer be adjusting Investment schedules; in order they may pay only what they wish, meaning as little as possible. Almost all Taxpayers would exclaim this is best, until they realize what is lost. Government tax revenues are vital, for payment of Government services. Taxpayers do not want elimination of these Government services. Effective Tax rates, or Deficit spending, remain the sole venues for payment for these Government services. A Tax Code as the Author here proposes, if it had been introduced in 1960; would have meant no National Debt past 1965, and a higher growth rate of GDP after 1970? Taxpayers should remember the adage: You have to spend Money, to make Money.

The above statement is based upon an estimate study of the Author's own. The parameters of the Study use model characteristics where Tax Code restrictions would again introduce Corporate Income tax into the matrix of importance contributions of Government tax revenues. The Author believes Corporate Income and Business taxes should compose at least half of all Tax revenues. The Reader must understand several serious considerations, before he jumps to the conclusion this practice constitutes a serious retardation of economic growth. Consumer Demand must be retained to for economic performance, and Boom conditions can only be excited by a switch to more expensive Substitute products by Consumers; they must buy Steak instead of Hamburger. This Substitute only develops easily, with a tax impact switch from tax on Consumer Income, to a tax on Business Profits. These Profits stand dependent on the foregoing Product substitution.

Corporate Income and Business taxes are a taxation of the Profits of Enterprise, these being Net Profits; denuded of all Expenses and previous taxes paid. Supply-Side Economists declare these Profits are necessary for Investment purposes. The Author disagrees. He has previously shown Capitalization remains funded by In-Step payments of the Production cycle. Taxes are assessed on Net Profits, which have already discounted the In-Step payments as Expense. Net Profits are derived from End-Sale of Product. Taxes incite Cost only after effective Recapitalization and Capitalization of future Production has already been funded and accounted. No loss of Capitalization should be endured by a more effective Tax Code.

Effective payment of the National Debt would have occurred by 1965, if Corporate and Business tax rates had been maintained from the early 1950s. Corporate and Business maximization of their tax exemptions would have brought higher hard capitalization of Production rates within two years of the implementation of Tax Code. Labor income would not only have risen because of the higher rate of hard capitalization, but their Discretionary Income would have increased in proportion to their Income, because of an effective discounting of their tax cost. The higher Consumption and Savings rates would have propelled more capital construction. The Author estimates hard capital construction would have been 14 percent higher in rates past 1970.

The above estimates are a direct repudiation of Supply-Side Economics, which believes Business should enjoy tax preferments and security from civil liability. It is also repudiation of Keynesian thought that Government debt fuels the Economy. The Author has shown there must be serious Unemployment of both Labor and Resources, for such fuel to be effective for economic growth, and then only if it propels provision of high-wage Jobs. It is certain that Capitalization is funded and accounted before the assessment of tax. The real impact of the Tax Code proposed will appear in the next Chapter, which seriously curtails the practice of internal financing by Corporate structures.

Chapter

American Corporations, or Corporations operating within the American economy, have utilized internal financing of Production since the 1960s. These Corporations have sought tax reductions and introduced Price schedules producing economic profits from Product sale, all in order to institute this internal financing. They entered the arena of Consumer Credit, to induce Consumers to buy Product at inflated Prices. Internally financed Production is conducted in a very sloppy manner at Corporate Board level, simply to escape potential tax of internally-held funds. Corporate internal financing of Production rarely utilizes the investigative studies utilized by the Banking industry; most Corporate Boards, who approve all Investment ventures, could not fill in a quarter of the information necessary for a proper Prospectus for a loan from a financial institution. The viability of internally-financed Production meets expectations, with such Production being over funded, Production capacity being too large for effective Consumer Demand, poor quality of produced Good, and eventual losses of Profit; these losses must be averaged with more profitable Production operations of the Corporation, to the detriment of Stockholder, laid-off Labor, and Consumer.

Effective Tax Provision can vastly alter the scenario presented, to the benefit of all, except poor Corporate management likely to be replaced with competent personnel:

> **Congress herein decrees Business organizations must advance all assessed Taxes within the Year following the Year of assessment. A special penalty of loss of all Tax deductions, exemptions, and credits will be imposed, if and when Profits of a previous year have not been distributed to Stockholders in the Year of Tax assessment following such non-distribution of Profits.**

> **Corporations which found Operations to provide Consumer Credit, or internal finance of Production operations, must register as a Banking institution subject to all the regulations imposed by Federal and State jurisdictions on Banking institutions. Such Banking institutions must reside on American soil, and be chartered by some American jurisdiction, in order for Government recognition of said institutions; Deposits will be**

construed as undistributed Profits of the Company, without this prior registration.

Such Banks must be in compliance with all Banking regulations within the jurisdiction of Operation. Bank shares must be held by the Stockholders of the Corporation, Stock Options of Bank stock can only be given to Bank officers—not Corporate officers exterior to the specific Credit institution, and loans of said Bank must conform to standard issuance policy as supervised by jurisdictional Banking commissions. Profits from the Credit institution must be distributed to Corporation Stockholders, as must be Withdrawals from the institution of Deposits by the Corporate management. All above criteria must be fulfilled, or these Deposits will be considered undistributed Profits, rendering loss of all Tax deductions, exemptions, and credits in the Year of definition for the Corporation.

The foregoing Tax Provision provides a great alteration from current Tax Policy, which will great even great amendment to current Business practice.

Corporations today hoard Profits, mostly earned from Price scheduling for Product, which provides economic Profits for the Corporation. This hoarding has various root causes, the majority being maintaining Corporate stock listing prices, allowing massive wealth transfers to Corporate management through Stock Options, and funding Consumer purchases from credit for greater Sales volume for Product lines. All three of these rationales have nothing to do with aggregation of Capital for expanding Production. They have to be examined.

The sole rationale for maintaining the Stock listing prices for Corporate stock, is to freeze the ordinary Stockholder out of greater share of the Corporate profits engendered in operation. Lower Dividend payments would bring call for replacement of Corporate management, with a more effective team, management desirous of keeping their position. Higher Stock Dividends would raise the price of the Stock listing eventually, and bringing calls for Stock Splits. This is an Issuance of Stock at some multiple of current Stock, and distributing the new Multiple of Stock to current Stockholders equally. This is direct participation of all Stockholders in the Profits derived from Production. Corporate managements desire to enrich themselves in their office; they do not intend to enrich ordinary Stockholders from Corporate operations, simply paying Stockholders a sufficient return to enjoin their purchase of Corporate stock.

Corporate management uses Stock Options and Stock Decrees to Corporate officers, for the purpose of transferring wealth from Corporate coffers to personal Corporate officer accounts. Corporate officers simply sell the Stock given by Stock Decree on the open market, or exercise their Stock Option; then sell it on the open market. They can also request the Corporation buy back the Stock, thereby not expanding outstanding Stock releases. Corporate officers gain the profits of the Corporation in either case.

The argument for Stock Options expounded states Stock Options pay remuneration to Corporate officers, which would be an extra burden to Corporate operations if paid in salary and benefits. It remains poor explanation for theft from Corporate Stockholders, when distress at direct salary and benefits provision hurts none but a few dozen Start-up Corporations per year. Direct Corporate regulation by Government might be in order.

The provision of Consumer Credit is done solely to entice Consumers to purchase Corporate product at excessive Prices. The practice produces some of the greatest inflationary pressures in the Economy, as Consumers struggle to pay off excess cost of both Product and Credit. It contains the worst depressant of Consumer Demand, as it absorbs huge amounts of Consumer Discretionary Income. Another possible place for Government regulation, but further implementation of Tax policy could be equally as effective a regulatory power:

> **Congress herein declares any Business organization which issues Stock Decrees or Stock Options, of current Stock value greater than the gifted Employee's current salary and benefits, will lose all Tax deductions, exemptions, and credits for the Period Year in which the bequest was made. Additional condition for the Bequest insists the gifted Employee must sell the Stock to the Business organization, said Stock being excluded from the open market for Ten (10) years. This condition will protect Stockholder equity, and maintain Government tax revenues derived from Capital Gains.**

> **Congress herein declares any Business organization must inform every Consumer of Business Product a declared Cost of Production, a declared Cost of Distribution and Retail, and a listed Product item Profit which the Corporation expects to garner; failure to abide and provide this information will lead to loss of Tax deduction, exemptions, and credits accruing to the Business organization in the Tax Period Year where this failure of information is discerned. Inaccurate information presentation is herein decreed Fraud, and Violators will be charged Fines up to One (1,000,000) per Incident, up to Three (3) years of imprisonment, or both.**

The evils of current Business practice lies constrained by the Tax Provisions. Stockholder equity has been protected from Corporate management greed. Consumers obtain a better understanding of the Product price makeup, to make an informed decision to consume. Inequities of reimbursement between Management, Employees, and Stockholders have been redressed.

Government Tax policy stands far more rational in expression, serving vital economic interests of all segments of society, while guaranteeing higher tax revenues to pursue Government services for the general Population. The Capitalization function has been found to be relatively untouched by the Tax policy; funded and accounted before taxation. Corporate management greed and malfeasance have been highlighted, and their ability to secure financial resources from Stockholder reimbursement stopped. Only one more area of wild exuberance in tax loss must be examined, before we turn to actual rates of Income tax.

Chapter

The American people have an innate fondness for foreign manufactured Products, as well as a vast need foreign raw materials—especially Oil. Business personnel and Economists excuse such addition, with claims of cheaper Product for Consumers, saying it increases Consumer Demand and Business Profits. The Author asks what such benefits cost in the long-run. He clearly perceives down-the-road real disadvantages to this level of importation. So follows the following Tax Provision:

> **Congress herein decrees the placement of a Two (2%) percent Infrastructure Utility tax upon all materials and Product imported into this Nation, for purposes of manufacture, Sale, or Consumption. Previous imposed Duties or Imposts shall remain.**

We found a return to Protectionism necessary, but an economically sound initiative, devised both to raise Government tax revenues, and to bring a discriminatory taxation toward foreign products within the American economy. Readers should follow the discussion, before automatically condemning the practice.

Justification for the tax finds ease of expression. The tax simply insists foreign products and materials pay the same degree of tax, as do Producers of American product on American soil. American Producers have to pay Property taxes, Excise taxes on necessary materials, Sales taxes on End-Consumer goods needed for production, and Business taxes on their Profits. American Producers must reflect Costs of Production and Cost of Taxation, in their establishment of Price schedules for their Products. Foreign Imports escape taxation, and escape the trap of paying for American Costs of Operation priced at American Costs of American Suppliers and Utilities, within the current Tax Policy. This gives foreign Imports some 14 percent advantage over American Products, without even considering the highly important element of Wage scale differentials. Some form of taxation on foreign Imports need be introduced.

A two percent tax on Imports at the Point of Entry will have multiple effects. It will first generate a huge revenue for Government, under the huge Importation levels currently operating. This revenue, when studied, impacts the Consumer in the correct arena, without contraction of his Discretionary Income, on limitation of options in its expenditure. The Consumer is left free to choose his own inter-mix of Products and Services, in the context of limited Budget.

Some Economists will insist the level of Import taxation is not sufficient to impact Consumer preference. The Author disagrees, stating that taxation at Point of Entry has progressive effects. Purchasers of Imports at Port of Entry have to deal with increased Imports cost. These Purchasers, thereafter, have to contend with American distribution costs, American Retail Costs, and all Profits markups from those activities. The Author believes a two percent tax on Imports at a POE, will bring a final Product cost to Consumers of a 17–21% increase over the Price of Product prior to taxation. The Consumer loses none of his Discretionary Income, but his options have been constrained.

Economists will insist the tax will curtail actual purchase of Product, with less Profitability for Business, and less satisfaction for the Consumer. The increase of Price for the Consumer of Imports will reduce the availability of Consumer Demand for those Products, of which the Author will agree. It must be noted, though, that competitive American Product will likely see increases of Sales at rates half of the Tax impact, at the minimum. The increased Production will sub-stitute Business Profits levels on an Economy-wide scale, and the increased tax revenues will reduce Consumer tax liabilities, this raising total Consumer Demand over the long term. The tax will mean a readjustment of Investment for Business interests, and simply rescheduling of Budget for Consumers.

A secondary effect of the Tax will seem insignificant in the immediacy, but will have long-term consequences. The total reduction in Trade volumes incited by the Tax, will reduce pressures on the Transportation industry. Reductions in the total Fuel use of importation will reduce the overall cost of Fuel in this Coun-try, along with the cost imposed by the volume of Importation. There will be declining construction of Transportation equipment, as the volume of Trade decreases, this bringing down Capitalization Costs within the Transportation industry, while hardly affecting the Labor employment rates in the industry. This reduction in Transportation costs will eventually bring reductions, or at least, no additional costs to mark up Consumer Prices. The Economy, because of eco-nomic efficiencies, will be more resilient; less impacted by variations of short-term Consumer Demand.

The American people must be weaned from their dependence on foreign Imports. Actual Production must be brought back to American soil, and actual efficiency of Production in terms of materials utilization must be enhanced. Both of these goals are achieved with this moderate tax on Imports; so moderate they may escape a Trade war, as foreign nations understand the need to limit American consumption of foreign products to preserve World economic stabilization.

The Economic argument of the 'economies of Place production' has decreased with the advent of technology. Japan is a prime example in establishment of industry without local raw materials. These materials have almost invariably less Transportation cost than do Finished Products, because of greater volume of transportable material in the same units; Finished Products need Packaging protection and storage braces, raw materials needing only bulkheads. The Future demand fuels economy.

The Economic argument of 'augmentation of technologies' also loses weight in the progress of the World economy. The Internet and Tourism cancel any concealment of technology advantage. The interchange of diagrams and Production notes can be almost instantaneous, with relatively minimal Transportation costs. Patent usage royalties will make up the Trade of the future, outside of raw materials, as it is far less costly than bulk transit of Finished Products.

There was wide Economic rejection of Protectionism after the Great Depression, many Economists seeing this Protectionism as a root cause of the Depression. Tariffs and Protectionism got a bad Rap as consequence. The real cause of the Depression was technological increases in total volume of produced Product, without an equal increase in Consumer Demand. Warehouses were overstocked in the interval without War, but Wages, Benefits, and Interest rates were not allowed to rise. Consumer Demand requires the Consumer have ability to purchase. They were not given the wherewithal to purchase. This phenomenon had nothing to do with Tariffs or Protectionism. Economists shortsightedly claim Producers were not allowed to move excess Product Overseas, but Consumer Demand was equally lacking there. It was also patently obvious that there existed easy technological spread between the developed nations during the Period prior and during the Depression. Free Trade could not have altered the course of the Great Depression.

The antagonism toward tariffs and Protectionism remains relatively stupid, even after years of Free Traders ranting at it. A balanced degree of Protectionism and tariffs holds as much economic advantage, as does demanded Safety requirements on Consumer Products, or malpractice liabilities for professional occupations. It is economic suicide to allow Portability of Production to foreign manufacture, when domestic production can be more economically beneficial. Tariffs must be introduced universally, though, else all have to rely on the economic acumen of the political process.

Universal application low Tariffs serve as the excellent vehicle for Protection. Importation of most economically viable foreign Products remains almost unaltered in purchase patterns. Less desirable foreign Products faces much stiffer domestic Product competition. The result of this competition means a shift to domestic production, which because of the increased Employment in the domestic economy, means functionally no drop in overall Consumer Demand. Domestic industry still must compete with Imports, and so increase Production efficiency. Economics, as Profession, needs some rediscovery.

Chapter

The discussion finally turns to suggested Tax rates, probably what the Reader wanted to evaluate from the First, rather than read a relatively boring monologue! There is a dichotomy placement of Tax on Income. Rates should be set on largesse of Income under a progressive tax system, but tax rates should only be placed on ability to pay. The Reader may not perceive the inherent division, though it is simple. The Tax rates need be applied according to the degree of economic participation, but such economic participation incites Costs of it's own; in addition to relative exterior Costs such as possession of Dependents, increased Costs from Health care and infirmity, and exterior Debt Load not associated with economic participation. Taxing raw Income becomes unfair, and an undue burden upon the Taxpayer.

Adjustment of Tax rates for the stipulated reasons also have properties of injustice, as the Taxpayer himself has options to vary the cost and impact of the foregoing liabilities. This causes a greater problem due to the fact greater economic participation allows for higher capacity to avoid Cost of such liabilities. Households of greater Capitalization also enjoy advantage over less Capitalized Households. Tax Schedules, on the other hand, become functionally ineffective and raise no revenue, under impact of defined exemptions. The purpose of the Tax system is lost, with insufficient revenues and discriminatory impact.

The answer to the above quandary lies in universal application tax exemptions, impacting upon all; tax rates set reflecting the ability to pay, based on level of economic participation. The result becomes sometimes confusing, but need clear declaration. The Tax legislator has a heavy burden; he has to raise revenue, without creating economic adversity; while maintaining the ability for all Taxpayers to economically participate. The Tax Provision presented here:

Congress herein decrees Income Tax rates shall be the following:

Less than $20,000 per Tax Year—Three (3%) percent of Adjusted Income
$20,000–$30,000 per Tax Year—Eight (8%) percent of Adjusted Income
$30,000–$50,000 per Tax Year—Twelve (12%) percent of Adjusted Income.

$50,000–$100,000 per Tax Year—Twenty (20%) percent of Adjusted Income
Above $100,000 per Tax Year Period—Twenty-five (25%) percent of Adjusted Income.

All Income which allows for Economic participation as an Independent element, with the advantages of Independence, shall be subject to the above Tax, without delineation of the source of said Income.

Adjusted Income will be such residue of Income remaining, after all Tax deductions, exemptions, and credits stipulated in this Code are removed from total Income, along with all verifiable Business or Employment expense normally incurred in Business or Employment operation. No other element shall be allowed to alter total Income, or the components to satisfy creation of Adjusted Income as stipulated; which in any way reduces the total of Tax liability by the Taxpayer.

The Tax rates derived effectively delineate, or not, the abilities of the Taxpayers to ameliorate the liabilities inherent because of Dependencies and adverse positioning. The rates were determined by degree of Capitalization of the Mean Households within each Tax bracket, the Mean level of Household debt—along with the average rate of repayment of that debt, the observed multiplicities of Income instruments available to the Mean Household of the bracket—to determine viability duration under condition of loss of Employment, and average Household holding of independent Capital Assets separate from Household mortgages.

Most Tax Analysts would state the Rate increases are too sharp, and more divisions should be added. Household Budget behavior does not deviate significantly within the proposed divisions, but actually do alter significantly between Rate brackets. Tax legislators must identify accurate rates of economic participation and debt levels. Tax rates must reflect real economic degrees of difficulty for Households. Cost of Living and Dependent exemptions are outlined to reduce pressures of transition. Household debt expansion to pay Income tax remains a low variable ratio and unlikely, and potentially necessary within the first $3000 dollars of transitional bracket Income. The above statement may seem like carping, and it could possibly be, but multiplication of Income brackets activates only decrease Government revenues, without providing significant help to Taxpayers.

The beauty of the Tax Code resides in the universal application of the Tax Code to all forms of Income. Delineation of types of Income insists on a separate Tax Schedule structure, producing a multiplicity of Deductions, Exemptions, and Credits. These retain the mark and fact of tax evasion. The greatest injury current to the American economy consists of tax evasion, or unjust tax impact on economic participants; the worst forms are legally allowed tax evasion grants of freedom from taxation. Sales taxes are the most regressive form of taxes ever devised, which function to forestall a rise of the Poor to middle-class status, by throwing the burden of Government Support services onto them. The Richest Income class and most powerful Business structures, do not even pay the percentage tax rates demanded of Working Poor and 'Mom and Pop' Stores.

Many Economists cannot understand the harm intrinsic within such a structure. It directly constricts Consumer Demand, along with reduction of the Standard of Living. It multiplies the cost of Government Services, as the Lower Incomes lose ability to withstand extraordinary Cost expenses. It artificially inflates Prices, and thereby reduces Consumption, because Business passes on the expense of Tax to Consumers; without accepting any of the burden of Taxes. The Wealthy equally suffer from such distortion of Tax Burden. Luxury Item production becomes the sole avenue of obtaining equitable Profit returns, but the luxury item Producers soon join the Wealthy classes; the total class of Wealth soon finds escalating Price increases in luxury items, this to finance the lifestyle of Producers rather than Cost of Production increases. The foundation of all the distress underwent, remains an unfair Tax Code which discriminates in tax impact.

The foregoing analysis can be proven immune to efforts to alter the matrix, without alteration of the Tax Code. Old methods of Production cannot fund the Profits necessary to maintain the Business Profits currently demanded, an increasing share of Consumers dropping into the economically participating Poor, if not the financial Poor. These Consumers lack both acquired Capitalization and Labor skills to generate an Income, which would allow for Consumption in the luxury item market. Production in Industries geared to supply of standard Goods for the Poor and Working Poor, must operate on marginal Profit ratios which will not support the Wealthy in their lifestyle. The luxury item market economy cannot survive, because it will not support Service personnel. Recapitalization of the American economy can only come withe recapitalization of the American Consumers; this requires revision of the Tax Code, to eliminate Tax adversity of impact.

Appendix A

Proposed Tax Code

Section A

The basic Federal form of Taxation will be an Income Tax. Income, for Individual or Business organization, will be any form of compensation of any type, which allows the entity to be an Economic Participant. The only exemptions will be Welfare transfer payments made by Government action, below a certain monetary maximum determined by Congress on a yearly basis. All levels of Government retain all right and power to impose further taxes as they feel fit, but such taxes will be seen as entity exemption from assessed Federal Income tax. The Federal Government reserves the right to provide additional Personal exemptions and tax credits to the all subject to taxation, as long as they are uniform in nature. Normal reductions of assessed Income tax will remain in force to allow for normal Business expenses and unusual circumstances for specific classes of Taxpayers.

All Income tax rates will be uniform for all entities, and determined by act of Congress, with consent of the President, or override of a Veto. Such Income tax rates will be determined once a year in the normal Budget passage process. The Federal government reserves the right to violate the uniformity of the exemption of subordinate level taxes, with supplanting percentage rates of exemption of subordinate taxes; if Congress determines a subordinate jurisdiction assesses taxes radically above the average or mean of all subordinate jurisdiction rates of taxation.

Section B

Special Fund Budgets will remain defined, but taxation for such Budgets will be integrated into the Income Tax and Income Tax rates. Congress will determine yearly, within Appropriations legislation, how much of the General Revenues shall be diverted to fund the Special Budgets.

Section C

Consumption taxation, including what is commonly known as Sales taxes, will not be allowed at the Federal level. Congress suggests lower Jurisdictions repeal all such taxes. Such forms of Taxation retard the flow of Consumption and Trade. Congress reserves the right to impose Excise taxes on specific Products, in order to raise revenue or limit consumption of such Products. Congress specifically requests inferior Jurisdictions to limit their taxation measures to Income taxation, Property taxation, and Excise taxation.

Section D

Congress herein decrees all Tax credits, exemptions, or deductions from the assessed tax are null and void except for the following:

1. A normal Recapitalization credit of Seven (7%) per year on all depreciation property utilized in a Business organization. Averaging Accounting procedures will be used in assessment, but cannot be shifted forward or backwards in Tax periods; declaration must be made in the Current Tax Assessment Period Year.

2. Any Household or Business can employ a Tax credit of no more than $20,000 per Assessment Period Year, if they can prove an equal Investment in the same year; this only if the Tax credit does not exceed Twenty (20%) percent of the assessed tax after all other deductions, in the Period Year of Taxation. Twenty (20%) percent of the assessed tax can be received in any Period Year, except the numeral amount cannot exceed $20,000 per Period Year, unless Congress should declare an alteration in the numeral amount maximum.

SECTION E

Congress herein revokes all Tax credits for Investment as previously allowed. The sole replacement as Tax credit for Investment will consist of a total deduction of all taxes paid by Employees of the Business in the preceding Year of Taxation to the U.S. Government, or to some subsidiary Jurisdiction within the land and territory of the United States. This numeral amount of deduction shall not exceed fifty (50%) percent of the estimated tax assessment, prior to the potential deduction.

SECTION F

Congress herein decrees Business organizations must advance all assessed Taxes within the Year following the Year of assessment. A special penalty of loss of all Tax deductions, exemptions, and credits will be imposed, if and when Profits of a previous year have not been distributed to Stockholders in the Year of Tax assessment following such non-distribution of Profits.

Corporations which found Operations to provide Consumer Credit, or internal finance of Production operations, must register as a Banking institution subject to all the regulations imposed by Federal and State jurisdictions on Banking institutions. Such Banking institutions must reside on American soil, and be chartered by some American jurisdiction, in order for Government recognition of said institutions; Deposits will be construed as undistributed Profits of the Company, without the prior registration.

Such Banks must be in compliance with all Banking regulations within the jurisdiction of Operation. Bank shares must be held by the Stockholders of the Corporation, Stock Options of Bank stock can only be given to Bank officers—not Corporate officers exterior to the specific Credit institution, and loans of said Bank must conform to standard issuance policy as supervised by jurisdictional Banking commissions. Profits from the Credit institution must be distributed to Corporation Stockholders, as must be Withdrawals from the institution of Deposits by the Corporate management. All above criteria must be fulfilled, or such Deposits will be considered undistributed Profits, rendering loss of all Tax deductions, exemptions, and credits in the Year of definition for the Corporation.

SECTION G

Congress herein declares any Business organization which issues Stock Decrees or Stock Options, of current Stock value greater than the gifted Employee's current salary and benefits, will lose all Tax deductions, exemptions, and credits for the Period Year in which the bequest was made. Additional condition for the Bequest insists the gifted Employee must sell the Stock to the Business organization, said Stock being excluded from the open market for Ten (10) years. This condition will protect Stockholder equity, and maintain Government tax revenues derived from Capital Gains.

Congress herein declares any Business organization must inform every Consumer of Business Product a declared Cost of Production, a declared Cost of Distribution and Retail, and a listed Product item Profit which the Corporation expects to garner; failure to abide and provide this information will lead to loss of Tax deduction, exemptions, and credits accruing to the Business organization in the Tax Period Year where this failure of information is discerned. Inaccurate information presentation is herein decreed Fraud, and Violators will be charged Fines up to One (1,000,000) per Incident, up to Three (3) years of imprisonment, or both.

SECTION H

Congress herein decrees the placement of a Two (2%) percent Infrastructure Utility tax upon all materials and Product imported into this Nation, for purposes of manufacture, Sale, or Consumption. Previous imposed Duties or Imposts shall remain.

SECTION I

Congress herein decrees Income Tax rates shall be the following:

Less than $20,000 per Tax Year—Three (3%) percent of Adjusted Income
$20,000–$30,000 per Tax Year—Eight (8%) percent of Adjusted Income
$30,000–$50,000 per Tax Year—Twelve (12%) percent of Adjusted Income.
$50,000–$100,000 per Tax Year—Twenty (20%) percent of Adjusted Income

Above $100,000 per Tax Year Period—Twenty-five (25%) percent of Adjusted Income.

All Income which allows for Economic participation as an Independent element, with the advantages of Independence, shall be subject to the above Tax, without delineation of the source of said Income.

Adjusted Income will be such residue of Income remaining, after all Tax deductions, exemptions, and credits stipulated in this Code are removed from total Income, along with all verifiable Business or Employment expense normally incurred in Business or Employment operation. No other element shall be allowed to alter total Income, or the components to satisfy creation of Adjusted Income as stipulated; which in any way reduces the total of Tax liability by the Taxpayer.

APPENDIX B

Constitutional Amendment

No legislation can be passed into law can be more than fifty book-length pages in length, must be in legible language which any college graduate could read and understand, and must be constrained to one topic; violation of any of the prior conditions will lead to automatic dismissal by Federal courts as unconstitutional.

2) Congress and President shall have until September 1 of each Year to pass into law a Budget for the current operating Year. Failure to do so by this date insists the Budget passed into law of the previous Year shall constitute the operating Budget of the Current Year, and no legislation passed into law by the current Congress and signed into law by President shall take effect until a new Budget has been passed with appointment of Appropriations for the passed Law.

3) The Supreme Court of the United States, or any inferior Federal Court appointed by the Supreme Court, shall review each Year Budget passed into law, along with any Tax legislation passed into law. These Courts are to declare unconstitutional any provision of these Acts, which violate the Civil Liberties of any Party, provide discrimination or favoritism of any Person of Group, or trans-ference Tax Burden on or off any Group in an unfair manner. This power is intent on elimination of specific items of injustice from legislation, without nulli-fying the entirety of the Acts in question.

APPENDIX C

Capitalization and In-Step Payments of Production

Production cycle process consists of steps in the Production outline. Materials are purchased, Capital Equipment is bought and installed, Labor is hired and trained, Product is produced, distribution of Product is conducted, and then Product is marketed. Subcontracted Parts may have been used in the actual Production. All of these Resources are paid for upon use. These are the In-Step Payments in the Production cycle. Production Profits are returned only upon End-Sale of the Product. The interim In-Step payments are made by focused financial capital of the original Enterprise, coming from Business Savings or, more likely, Operating Credit from a financial institution.

Examination of the above conditions highlights an important aspect of the original Enterprise. Capitalization and Recapitalization have already been paid, before the End-Sale of the Product. All Subcontractors—be they Suppliers of materials, Equipment, Labor, Distribution facilities, or Marketing efforts—all have been paid upon completion of their part in the Production cycle. These Subcontractors, upon receipt of funds from their participation, immediately recapitalize their ability to supply Product service; or capitalize in greater degree, to be able to supply more Product service. Funds, which are not utilized for this immediate recapitalization, are left in some financial form for storage or future consumption.

This fact negates the use of Tax credits for the aggregation of Capital. Effective Recapitalization and Capitalization of Production sectors which provide service to the Production cycle have already been accounted as Expense, and funded. This is done prior to the actual Sale of End-Product, though all supplied services were End-Product of the Suppliers. The next relevance to the discussion consists in the fact Production Suppliers each possess their own Production cycle, with necessary In-Step payments to their Suppliers, who make their own Capitalization and Recapitalization decisions upon receipt of payment.

End-Product Sale is the source of all return of Capital and Recapitalization expense. It is not the source of Capital and Recapitalization decisions, which are made upon receipt of In-Step payments in the Production cycle. It is immaterial that they Payments are one and the same! These decisions are taken, funded, and accounted before Contractor sale of End-Product. The final and funding Contractor is the Consumer, who provided funds for Capital return.

Decisions to Capitalize or Recapitalize are made prior to End-Consumer supply of funds to Profits return for Capitalization. These decisions are accounted and funded by In-Step payments of the Production cycle, from the focused Funds of previous Capitalization. The function of Capital aggregation is accomplished by the In-Step Payments of the Production cycle. Capitalization and Recapitalization Accounting and Funding comes from the Production cycle itself. Tax or non-Tax of the Profits of Production is immaterial to aggregation of Capital. The Production cycle produces its recapitalization.

Consumer Demand stands as the primary drive of Capital accumulation. The more rapid the purchase of End-Product, the swifter the completion of the Production cycle. The swifter purchase of Product demands swifter recycling of Production. The rapidity of the Production cycle itself, determines not only the quicker In-Step Payments made within the Production cycle; but the degree of Capitalization and Recapitalization—based upon the expected volume of service supply Demands exhibited. This convoluted reasoning simply states Profits from Production incite Entrepreneur engagement in the Production of Product, but does not determine actual Capitalization or Recapitalization decisions, which are based upon In-Step payments.

Tax credits are functionless in Capital aggregation. Decisions for Capitalization or Recapitalization find base in expected future demand for Product, and are paid by In-Step payments. Decision-makers made their decisions based upon Capital funding costs, Profit ratios for Product production, and estimated Demand for the Product. All of these decisions are made before implementation of taxes. Capital aggregation derives from In-Step payments as well, as Funds as stored in financial instruments. The rate of Interest on Capital funding remains unaffected by Tax or non-Tax, especially non-Tax based upon discriminatory Tax Credits for Investments, which express favoritism for certain forms of economic activity. Tax Credits for Investment exist only to service the desires of Individual and Households, who possess resources with which to conform to the economic behavior pattern demanded, for usurious expansion of their total wealth.

0-595-30648-9